The Pink Palace REVISITED

BEHIND CLOSED DOORS AT THE BEVERLY HILLS HOTEL

Sandra Lee Stuart
and John Prince

BARRICADE BOOKS INC.
FORT LEE, NEW JERSEY

Published by Barricade Books Inc.
1530 Palisade Avenue
Fort Lee, NJ 07024

Distributed by Publishers Group West
4065 Hollis
Emeryville, CA 94608

Printed in the United States of America.

Library of Congress Cataloging-in-Publication Data

Stuart, Sandra Lee.
   The pink palace revisited: behind closed doors at the Beverly Hills Hotel / Sandra Lee Stuart and John Prince.
   ISBN 0-942637-84-4
   1. Beverly Hills Hotel. I. Prince, John II. Title
   TX941.B48S78 1993
   647.94794'9401—dc20
                                        92-36512
                                        CIP

0 9 8 7 6 5 4 3 2 1

to Carole,

the unescorted woman trying to enter the Polo Lounge,

without whom there would have been no book.

acknowledgements

We'd like to extend many thanks to all those who were so generous with their time and recollections for both this edition and the first one. Special thanks go to Ernest Brown, who for so many years made the Beverly Hills Hotel the special place it was, and to Kay Pick, that whirlwind extraordinaire.

John Prince
Sandra Lee Stuart

chapter one

Sunset Boulevard wraps its way from downtown Los Angeles twenty miles before it reaches the Pacific Ocean. Along the way it passes Hollywood, West Hollywood and the motel where Jim Morrison of the Doors once hung from a balcony several stories up. It becomes the famous Strip on which Tower Records cozies up to the many music producers who have offices nearby. Past Hamburger Hamlet, where there was once a bridle path, Sunset is transformed into the bisect of Beverly Hills, fabulous mansions line either side, conjuring up visions of Gloria Swanson and William Holden face down in her pool.

There, in the midst of this residential splendor, surrounded by sixteen acres of Southern California's most beautiful foliage and gardens, sits a grand legend, a pink piece of Americana. The Beverly Hills Hotel.

A building can be famous solely for its architecture, but usually it is interesting and important because of where it is and what has happened in it. The Eiffel Tower in the middle of an Iowa cornfield would draw some attention, but millions wouldn't climb its steps if they weren't rewarded at the top with the sight of Paris spread out below them. The White House might merit a glance or two, but not long lines of people wanting to tour it if Abraham Lincoln hadn't slept there in his especially constructed long bed, and John-John Kennedy hadn't played under the desk in the Oval Office.

There are some places, like the White House and the Roman Colosseum, so intertwined with history, we go to soak it in and become a part of what has come before.

But history is not all wars and assassinations and coronations. It is the fabric of our past woven to unify us. We shared a common yesterday, therefore we can go forward into a common tomorrow. There are facets of history—which is really only gossip, according to Oscar Wilde—that may be trivial and silly, but nevertheless captivate and fascinate us.

The Pink Palace on Sunset Boulevard has played hostess and kept the secrets of the most famous and infamous personages of the twentieth century. It has witnessed the rise and fluorishing of America's favorite industry—the movies. It has seen romances start, marriages end, megadeals forged, and conspiracies collapse.

The city of Beverly Hills formed around it in the teens. The Vanderbilts sat on its porches in the twenties. Carole Lombard and Cesar Romero skated down its driveway in the thirties. Loretta Young owned it in the forties. Ava Gardner graced its pool in the fifties. Elizabeth Taylor lived in its bungalows in the sixties. John Lennon and Yoko Ono checked in in the seventies. Ivan Boesky wrested control of it in the eighties.

The history of this hotel has paralleled and comingled with that of the country, making it worth a visit, as you shall see as you tiptoe past the closed doors of the Beverly Hills Hotel.

chapter two

Even at its geologic beginnings, Southern California showed a quirky rebelliousness, a determination to do as it pleased.

As other land masses, mountains, canyons, hills, and ravines twisted, heaved, folded, and faulted to sculpture the earth's surface, Southern California would pop out of the ocean, be terra firma for a while, then slip back underwater. The best guess is the Los Angeles area first appeared one hundred and sixty million years ago, give or take a few hundred millenia.

Thousands of years later, at about the time flowering plants began to bloom, uneasy gurglings in the earth formed the granite core of the Santa Monica Mountain chain. The Santa Monica is a picturesque ridge running from Pasadena in the east across to the Pacific, providing present-day homeowners in Beverly Hills, Bel Air, and the Pacific Palisades with their multimillion dollar views.

Even with the anchor of the mountains' granite core, Southern California continued its frolic in the surf and resubmerged. Finally a powerful volcano let out a tremendous belch and forced the land out of the ocean once and for all, where it has remained ever since, despite periodic attempts to earthquake itself back into the Pacific.

During the Pliocene or Miocene epochs, about fifty or sixty million years ago, oil was formed and trapped in the area. The black gold, wide beaches, balmy temperatures, and sunny skies would prove to be strong and seductive magnets.

Fast, fast forward through time to Humanity.

It is not certain from where the North American Indians originally came, across the Bering Straits and down from Alaska or up from South America, but it is known that Shoshoneans were in Southern California by the time the Spanish conquistadors turned their acquisitive eyes in that direction.

California was a newer land in a new land. Peru, Mexico, the Caribbean had been divvied up. Late-arriving conquerors had to find new sources of booty. For that reason, on August 2, 1769, the Spanish governor of the Californias, Captain don Gaspar de Portola, and a band of companions bedded down at a small river some one hundred miles north of San Diego at a spot where, according to all records, no European had bedded down before.

The group called their campsite *Pueblo de Nuestra Senora la Reina de los Angeles de Porcincula*, in anticipation of the village that they hoped would someday be there. Luckily for future cartographers and ticket agents, the name was shortened to *Los Angeles*.

The next day's trek brought the explorers to a thick grove of sycamores with a watercress-lined stream meandering through it. They set up tents, with no way of knowing or even dreaming that a century and a half later, other men would also erect shelter there for overnight travelers. The later one would have wall-to-wall carpeting, feather pillows and linen sheets, hot and cold running water, marble bathtubs, a swimming pool constantly warmed to seventy degrees, dining rooms, banquet halls, maids, butlers, bellhops, waiters, and other luxuries that don Gaspar could only have believed possible in heaven, if he could have imagined it at all.

The Spaniards called this second campsite the Spring of the Sycamores of Saint Stephen (a third-century pope and the patron saint of bricklayers). This name, unshortened, stuck until the land became the property of Maria Rita Valdez.

Maria Rita received Spring of the Sycamores in a land grant of 4,539 acres in either 1831 or 1841. (The grant says 1831, but the governor who signed it wasn't in office until 1841.) Maria Rita changed the name to *Rodeo de las Aguas*, ranch of the gathering waters, in deference to the torrents that cascaded down nearby canyons during the rainy season, turning a good portion of her spread into marshland.

Capitalizing on her good fortune proved difficult. The logical use for the land was cattle ranching, which Maria Rita tried. She was hit with drought, Indians of an unfriendly persuasion, and her cantankerous relative, Luciano Valdez, who had also been named in the grant. Their trouble started when Luciano built his house too close to Maria Rita's red-tiled adobe one. When she complained, he retaliated by driving her cattle from the watering hole. Unable to resolve their differences, Luciano and Maria Rita took their dispute to the Los Angeles City Council. It was decided that Maria Rita should buy out Luciano—for $17.50. (One hundred and fifty years later, two acres of her spread sold for $13.5 million.)

Even without Luciano, the going continued to be rough. In 1852 several of Maria Rita's neighbors were killed in an Indian raid. Two years later when a couple of enterprising Yankees, Benjamin Davis Wilson and Major Henry

Hancock, offered her four thousand dollars, Maria Rita was more than ready to accept the money and walk out of the history books. Wilson was a colorful character who, among other things, founded California's orange industry and commercial vineyards, was the first Indian agent for Southern California, was a state senator, and had a mountain— Mount Wilson—named after him.

He and Hancock fared little better than their predecessor. Planting two thousand acres of wheat, they reaped a harvest of debts. They, too, were plagued by drought, more drought, and, to add insult to injury, flood.

After Wilson sold, the land passed from owner to owner and failure to failure. Because oil had been found in nearby La Brea, a company called Pioneer Oil acquired *Rodeo de las Aguas* and began drilling in the mid-1860s. It came up dry.

A few years later, E. A. Benedict and his son, Pierce, bought 3,608 acres of the ranch for $10,775. A company, the De Las Aguas Land Association, was formed and much of the ranch was divided into 75-acre lots. No one was interested in buying.

By the time the Los Angeles-Pacific Rail Road ("The only double track to the ocean") got around to putting up a blink-of-the-eye depot, christened "Morocco Junction," in 1879, the property was being used for sheepherding and not much else. The station brought new hopes. People began envisioning a thriving community growing up around it. Of course, people were envisioning thriving communities growing up all over Southern California.

The 1880s marked the beginning of a land boom dubbed The Iowa Influx. Incredible numbers of Easterners and Middle Americans were making a lemming-like drive across the country to the Pacific. Once there, they were met by carney-barking speculators and would-be developers eager to sell them homes in new "towns."

These "towns," often little more than plats and titles, were popping up wherever a sign could be pounded into the ground, often in highly undesirable and near-unbuildable locations. Developers, using the tactics of snake-oil salesmen, attempted to pass off disadvantages as assets. Deserts became health spas. Mountain-goat slopes offered marvelous views. Desolate areas became refuges from the madding crowd, and swamps were harbors.

It was hyperbole taken to crazy heights, with freak shows, bands, elephants, and free lunches.

Between 1884 and 1888, one hundred of these towns were platted in Los Angeles County alone. Signs were erected for Sunset, Hyde Park, Ivanhoe, Border City, Chicago Park, Ferondale, Hesperia, Gladysta, Englewood (which promised "no fog, no frosts, no alkali, no adobe"), Ballona, Bethune, Minneapolis, Terracina, Walteria, Rosecrans. Of the one hundred, only thirty-eight went beyond developers' sales spiels and were actually built.

Who, after all, would want to buy land in Border City, described as being "most accessible by means of balloon, and...as secure from hostile invasion as the homes of cliff-dwellers. Its principal resource...a view of the Mojave Desert"? Apparently no one did. Bust followed boom.

By the turn of the century, developers began learning from their mistakes. A few miles east of Morocco Junction, a company using a fair amount of imagination and common sense decided that sales spiels and brochures were not enough to get potential buyers to sign on the dotted line.

Most people are not good at visualizing. Buyers need three dimensions, something solid. The developers of this town-to-be, which they named Hollywood, would follow the lead of Los Angeles and market their town as a piece of goods. As one observer wrote, Los Angeles was "not a mere city. On the contrary it is, and has been since 1888, a commodity; something to be advertised and sold to the people of the United States like automobiles, cigarettes and mouth washes."

Accordingly, before the first customer was allowed on the site, Hollywood's developers laid out streets, planted trees, built an imposing bank building and a hotel—the Hollywood Hotel, appropriately enough—which was decorated and staffed. To add to the effect, bricks, sand, lumber, and other construction odds and ends were hauled onto lots and fake *SOLD* signs were put up. Deception? No more than most, good, old American advertising. It's the "nine out of ten doctors use Dristan or Drano or whatever" syndrome. If it's good enough for all those doctors, it must be good enough for me. If someone else has bought a house in this Hollywood place, maybe I should, too.

In any case, the planning, attention to detail, and the special steam trains that chugged up from Los Angeles on opening day to be met in Hollywood by brass bands, quickly paid off, giving the developers a 60 percent profit.

A few miles west, Morocco Junction was not enjoying similar success. Instead of brass bands and bustling communities, the train station there was surrounded by lima beans.

In 1900, another oil company, undaunted by Pioneer Oil's experience twenty-five years earlier, bought up land around Morocco Junction. This one, Amalgamated Oil, brought in drills, sank bits, and miracle of miracles, made a strike.

They were unable to drill deep enough to hit oil, but they did find water.

Water may not be as good as oil, nonetheless, it was a valuable product, especially in that part of Southern California. Bowing to its assets, Amalgamated Oil changed its name to the Rodeo Land and Water Company and waited for the money to roll in. It didn't. It's one thing to have a product and another to find someone who wants it. And the few farmers, shepherds, and squatters around Morocco Junction didn't.

It was obvious, at least to Rodeo's president, Burton Green, that measures would have to be taken to attract ongoing customers. The days of making millions selling water a bottle at a time were yet to come. Green was looking for customers who used water every day—for drinking, cooking, bathing, and laundering. The way to get them was to build a town. It didn't matter to him that others had already failed at turning Maria Rita's cattle ranch into a prosperous community. He was imbued with that myopic brashness that was so much a part of the American character and spirit.

If we as a nation hadn't pushed on with our impossible dreams and improbable schemes, believing deeply in our manifest destiny and that anything could be accomplished with American grit and know-how, we would have long ago thrown up our hands and accepted the fact that this country is ungovernable, the ingredients in our pot will never melt together, and there is no reason in the world why we've lasted as long as we have. But our land-of-opportunity psyche compels us to ignore the odds and try again. Not only would Burton Green build a town, he would do so on a grand scale.

He wouldn't settle for some Podunk for pipefitters. Green wanted a gracious, stylish town with wide boulevards, lovely parks, and lots of trees, as Baron Haussmann had given Paris when he redesigned it. Green especially wanted trees. He ended up hiring a landscape architect from New York to plan the residential areas where streets would be lined with palms, maples, magnolias, oaks, and elms. (Trees became so ingrained in the city's heritage that the city council was later to spend three full years haranguing and fighting over what was to be planted along Wilshire Boulevard. The palm narrowly defeated the rubber tree.)

It was decided that *Morocco* was too gaudy a name for what Green hoped would be a solid, affluent community. He chose instead the more staid-sounding *Beverly Hills*, the "Beverly" being for the Massachusetts farm where President Taft vacationed and "Hills" because there were some.

In 1907 the subdivision was officially recorded with the proper authorities. A Mr. Henry C. Clarke built the town's first house, on Crescent Drive. There was no rush to follow him. Contrary to expectations, by 1910 only a disappointing six houses had been built north of Santa Monica Boulevard, a street running parallel to the steam-train tracks.

It looked like another bust. The trees, attractively laid-out streets, even the accessibility to water, weren't enough.

By 1914, Beverly Hills was still population hungry. When it came time to incorporate, it lacked the requisite five hundred residents. The Rodeo Land and Water Company had to temporarily relocate some of its Mexican workers across the town line from West Hollywood.

If Burton Green was not to be one more failed entrepreneur, he had to come up with something to make his Beverly Hills work. He needed to merchandise his town as they had Hollywood; he needed a come-on, a lure, the prize in the Cracker Jack box.

He needed a Pink Palace.

chapter three

It was an unlikely place to put a hotel. There wasn't much there and not much to do other than watch the lima beans grow. Burton Green's friends advised him to call it quits. Doing anything more with the property would be throwing good money after bad. But Green was an inveterate gambler, a wildcatting oilman in the days before cost-controlling accountants insinuated themselves into the industry. Big risks lead to big payoffs. He was not about to give up before placing one more big bet on the roll of the die.

Green would not be dissuaded by the very sound arguments that another hotel was not needed, especially not in Beverly Where? There were already several fine establishments in downtown Los Angeles. The nascent movie colony had their own hotel in Hollywood, and bluebloods looking for a touch of Boston had the elegant Raymond in Pasadena.

Furthermore, the area had a number of resort hotels that could boast of scenic beauties that a hotel in Beverly Hills couldn't hope to match. The Santa Monica Mountains were lovely, but they weren't the Alps. And they certainly weren't worth traveling three thousand miles to see. How could Green's hotel compete with the magnificent Del Coronado overlooking the Pacific in San Diego or the equally beautiful Arlington, up the coast in Santa Barbara? These were true resorts with tennis courts, horseback riding, surf parties, picnics, hunting trips, and other more contrived activities such "flora-and-fauna expeditions."

Edmund Wilson was one critic who rhapsodized over the Del Coronado, which was placed on the National Register of Historic Places in 1971. "Airy, picturesque, and half-bizarre, it is the most magnificent example extant of the American seaside hotel as it flourished...on both coasts. White and ornate as a wedding-cake, polished and trim as a ship, it makes a monument not unworthy to dominate the last blue concave dent in the shoreline before the United States gives way to Mexico."

Even if he lacked oceans, beaches, and scenic wonders, Green was determined to compete. He would create his own wonder, plant his own scenery. He would build a palace, one that would be at the same time grand and comfortable, gracious and lovely. It would be a place where prospective mansion-buyers would feel at home and be put in the buying frame of mind.

The hotel's construction was a local curiosity. Children from neighboring ranches rode over to watch the progress. Los Angelenos would make a Sunday outing of braving the rutty roads to picnic next to the site.

What they saw was certainly a sight. T-shaped, arched, cupolaed, the hotel's three stories began to dominate the landscape until they were the landscape, shrinking the mountains and hills behind them. It was designed in a bastard style, variations of which have been called "Moorish," "Spanish mission," and "Spanish colonial," although architect Frank Lloyd Wright more tartly referred to it as tawdry Spanish medievalism.

Wright did not think much of Southern California architecture in general, dismissing it as an "eclectic procession to and fro in the rag-tag cast-off the ages." Usually natural conditions, such as climate and building materials, dictate what gets built in a certain area. Just as almost anything can be grown in Southern California, anything can be built—as long as you don't let taste and common sense get in the way.

The Iowans who traveled west no sooner left their flat plains than they were hit with nostalgia. To alleviate homesickness, they built small-roomed houses that, according to one historian, "bulged out with a bunion in the way of a bay-window. Coming out nearly as far as the bay-window was a tiny porch. The Iowans had pleasant visions of sitting on the front porch in the long tropical evenings. They found that night followed day as suddenly as the dropping of a curtain, without romantic twilight, and that the evenings, even in summer, were so cold that they would have to muffle themselves in their buffalo overcoats."

The usually sensible and down-to-earth New Englanders who migrated to the Los Angeles area were little better. They were accustomed to battling the vagaries of Nature, like wind, snow, flood. They built their California houses with sloped roofs, as they did back in Massachusetts and Maine, to keep piled snow from causing cave-ins, and they dug cellars for furnaces they would not need.

Frank Lloyd Wright notwithstanding, at least Spanish-Moorish-mission style looked like it belonged in its surroundings. It became popular, a rage actually, after the 1915 Panama-California Exposition in San Diego. The city fathers had proposed the fair as a way of promoting the virtues of their town in hopes of attracting businesses and residents. To their dismay, they learned that San Francisco was planning an exposition with a similar theme at the same time. In an attempt to draw visitors south, the San Diego planners came up with the gimmick of designing all their exhibit buildings in the same white-stucco, ocher-tiled-roof style.

Soon it seemed like everyone wanted to "go Spanish," although it was a Spanish that Goya or Cervantes would have had trouble recognizing. The entire city of San Clemente was nothing but acres and acres of white stucco and ocher tiles.

The Beverly Hills Hotel, a precursor of this craze, was built in a pseudo-mission style, with thick walls that captured the night's coolness and held it, with a slight mildewy dampness, throughout the heat of the day. There were large public areas and small guest rooms in the main building, as was then the custom.

In contrast, rooms in the ten detached bungalows were spacious. The parlors were large enough to accommodate grand pianos. The bungalows were meant to be comfortable temporary residences for people who were used to living on a grand scale. King Gillette, of razor blade fame and fortune, occupied one while his mansion was being built.

There was one extremely noticeable departure from the Spanish mission style, though it is not known to whom the credit for the idea should given. At some point someone decided that instead of white stucco, the Beverly Hills Hotel would be painted an unbelievable, stand-out, signature pink—a pink that at times is salmon, other times rose, and at a certain twilight moment, the exact color of the western sky. (The occasional unromantic person has seen it as Kaopectate pink.)

In 1912 when the buildings were all completed and the gardens planted, Burton Green had spent five hundred thousand dollars on his big gamble. The question was, would it pay off or would it be one more monument to unbridled American optimism?

Green was realistic enough to realize that he didn't know how to manage a hotel. Hotels are very peculiar enterprises. Green, a Wisconsin immigrant, was a businessman with neither the temperament nor inclination to make a hotel work. What sets a great hotel apart from mediocre ones is not so much the physical amenities—the beds and bathrooms—as it is the service and the character the staff gives it. Great hotels have an intangible essence that set them apart.

What Green needed was someone who could breathe life and character into his establishment, someone to set the desired tone and at the same time be a superior manager. Luckily for him, he didn't have to go far to find just such a person.

Four and a half miles to the northeast, between Highland and Orchid Avenues, sat the very successful Hollywood Hotel. Its manager was Mrs. Margaret Anderson, a matronly, gracious woman with a gift for saying the right word and providing the appreciated gesture and touch to make even the most demanding guests happy. The Hollywood Hotel owed its success to her. She could obviously attract and keep the type of guest that Green was seeking. Unfortunately for him, she was quite content at the Hollywood.

When Green initially approached Mrs. Anderson, her friends were quick to counsel her to refuse. After all, she was not only running a well-established and lucrative hotel, she also held the lease on it. A move to Beverly Hills would mean giving up her security, and for what? As charming and grand as the buildings and grounds were, she would be starting over again, with all the attendant worries, work, and frustrations.

But Burton Green held a trump card. He had never wanted to be in the hotel business. The hotel was merely a means to his real estate ends. So he had no compunctions in offering Mrs. Anderson not only the managership and a lease, but also an option to buy at a price that could only be considered a giveaway.

Being the practical woman she was, Mrs. Anderson accepted.

Opening a new hotel, under the best and most thought-out circumstances, can be a harrowing experience. Many owners and managers suffer anxiety attacks on that first day, overcome by the fear, sometimes justified, that the doors will swing open and no one will step inside. There was one hotelier who had sunk most of his fortune into building a magnificent resort complex in Jamaica. A man with vast knowledge of the business, who was prone to leaving little to chance, he had spent weeks coaching, scolding, and training his staff on the intricacies and specifics of caring for and pampering guests accustomed to the best. His kitchens and bars were stocked with only the finest foods, delicacies, wines, and liqueurs.

He invited many of his jet-setting, European-society friends to a party on the day after the opening, assuming that most of them would fly in the day before. It was only after he received all the responses that he realized all the invitees were arriving only hours before partytime. When the doors were officially thrown open to welcome guests, only one, portly lady showed up.

The owner watched, bemused, as three overeager doormen almost carried the lady to the front desk. As she was signing the register, an unsettling thought occurred to him. The only guest, after freshening up in her room, would undoubtedly make her way to the cocktail lounge for a drink. How uncomfortable it would be for her to sit tippling by herself as the waiters hovered nearby.

Obviously this was unacceptable. The owner quickly rounded up some staff members, dressed them in suitable attire, and planted them in the bar, drinks in hand. By the time the lady came down, the cocktail lounge was buzzing at a convivial pitch.

The lady had a dry martini. She had another. She was ordering her third when something else occurred to the owner. The lady wasn't going to drink forever. Surely she must be approaching her limit and soon would be changing venue to the dining room, which, of course, was empty except for its crew of expectant waiters. Unobtrusively, he directed the imbibing staff members, who were very much enjoying their first night on the job, to move to the restaurant. By the time the bona fide guest wobbled in, they were perusing the menu and ordering dinner.

Finally, the dessert course was served and eaten, and the one and only guest retired to her room. The owner poured himself a stiff drink and toasted to better—and more profitable—days to come.

May 12, 1912, the opening day of the Beverly Hills Hotel held no similar calamities for Mrs. Anderson. She had carefully planned and mapped out the day with the precision of General Norman Schwarzkopf's ground attack on Iraq.

The primary objective for Mrs. Anderson was the comfort of her guests—one hundred from the Hollywood Hotel saw no reason to stay there if Mrs. Anderson was leaving. Most of the Hollywood's staff followed her as well—Mrs. Hudson, the housekeeper; Mrs. Mary Parry, the linen-keeper; Wilbur, the gardener; and Harry, the headwaiter. In addition to this army, most of the Hollywood's furnishings, which Mrs. Anderson owned, had to be moved.

The guests breakfasted at the Hollywood, while maids busily packed their belongings, and lunched at the Beverly Hills, while maids unpacked their belongings.

This was how Mrs. Anderson did things—meticulously, methodically, and well. From day one, the Beverly Hills Hotel exemplified its manager—dignified, sedate, and ready for bed at ten. Mrs. Anderson's clientele was the Blue Book rich, the carriage-trade elderly who checked in for weeks and months at a time. These were people who "summered" and "wintered" and traveled with valets; people who disliked ostentation, deplored vulgarity, and expected a fingerbowl between courses; people who liked Mrs. Anderson and whom she liked.

And most importantly, these were people that Burton Green liked.

In later decades the image of Southern California would become that of a haven for musclebuilders and would-be starlets whose ages and IQs were roughly equivalent. It would be where people believed that humming would bring inner peace, or, if that didn't work, then screaming that you hate your mother for several hours would. "Normal" people in Omaha would look upon it with indulgence, as an adult might an unpredictable and cute child. The fact is that Southern California, despite some fringe groups drawn mostly by the movie and music industry, is as stable and steady as, say, New England. It's just warmer. Furthermore, despite its reputation for beach bunnies and surfers, the area had a large population of retirees. It was the St. Petersburg of the Southwest.

This was the market Burton Green was after. He wanted wealthy retirees, or near-retirees, to be the core of his Beverly Hills. Mrs. Anderson was bringing such people to the hotel. They came for a visit, liked what they saw, and gradually began buying lots and houses.

In those early days, Beverly Hills was uncrowded and leisurely. Early residents remember it as "lovely" and quiet. A trip downtown on a warm Saturday afternoon could mean being totally alone on the street—no other people or any cars to be seen.

Actually, to paraphrase Gertrude Stein, there wasn't much there to downtown Beverly Hills, only a depot, a drugstore, and a furniture shop. Even as late as 1924, the town was so undeveloped that on hot days, the few stores and offices in the central business district had to close to avoid heavy clouds of dust churned up by workers in nearby bean fields.

To give the illusion of more substance, and to make sure people knew where they were, the city fathers planted a vibrant array of greenery and flowers at the depot. One clump was arranged to spell out *Beverly Hills.* (Years later this flowery welcome was abandoned after mischievous vandals with an editorial bent kept pulling out strategic blossoms so the display read *Beverly Ills.*)

The landscaping went from the station, along Rodeo Drive, to the hotel; the same route taken by the one-car trolley that shuttled guests and domestics in the early years. The original shuttle was a rickety Model T that had to be replaced after an amorous Great Dane knocked it over. When the trolley line was discontinued because more and more people became auto oriented, the tracks were converted into a bridle path by Mrs. Anderson's son Stanley and several other civic- and scenic-minded locals. A white-haired, elegant character actor named Hobart Bosworth regularly rode his stallion along the "Ye Bridle Path." He was gazed upon by the impressionable pubescent girls of the time with much the rapture that a Luke Perry gets today. Years later one of Bosworth's admirers remembered that "Everyone came to Beverly Hills to see that man ride his horse."

Before long there were other reasons to come to Beverly Hills. One by one mansions were being built in the hills and more modest homes on the flats. The population ballooned from seven hundred in 1920 to seventy-five hundred in 1925. In 1921 the first edition of the Beverly Hills city directory was issued. There were only four listings for the hotel:

Anderson, Stanley	Beverly Hills Hotel 603 04
Beverly Hills Hotel	Sunset Boulevard 603 04

Beverly Hills Hotel Garage Beverly Hills Hotel 559 106
Moore, Tom   Beverly Hills Hotel 604 04

Contributing to this population explosion was something that would establish Beverly Hills and make realtors happy from then on. That something was the house Doug built for Mary.

This particular Doug was Douglas Fairbanks, the exuberant swashbuckler of the silent screen. The Mary was Mary Pickford, dubbed America's Sweetheart by Thomas Edison and stuck with that nickname for the rest of her life. Their romance had all the makings of a wonderful, true-life love story—he dashing and handsome, she sweet and fragile. Instead it was a scandal ready to erupt. Pickford and Fairbanks were both married to other people. To make matters worse, Mrs. Fairbanks was a friend of Mary's. She would be in the kitchen seeing to dinner, while Doug and Mary were holding hands in the parlor.

Moral sensibilities have changed so much in our country over the last century that it is difficult to imagine how such a popular figure as Mary Pickford could be so afraid of public reaction to her affair. In the nineties, eyebrows were raised when it was revealed that Woody Allen had taken up with longtime lover Mia Farrow's twenty-one-year-old adopted daughter. Allen did take some editorial heat for cradle-robbing lack of sensitivity. He was not, however, burned in effigy. With Madonna making a fortune out of publicly clutching her crotch, it takes more than marital impropriety to elicit national moral outrage.

Things were very different seventy years ago. The state of matrimony was, at least in theory, still sacrosanct, and divorce carried social scorn and shame with it—even though 150,000 couples *were* divorced in 1919.

According to Pickford's biographers, she feared social reaction to a break-up of her marriage and so stayed married even though the relationship was over.

Fairbanks, perhaps because his public persona was so different from Pickford's, went ahead and got a divorce. He then went househunting, apparently certain that some day he and Mary Pickford would be married. When that happened, he didn't want to live in the same house she had shared with her previous husband, even though Grayhall was not at all shabby. (King of the Suntan, George Hamilton was living in Grayhall when he made headlines by escorting Lynda Baines Johnson to the Academy Awards presentations.)

Fairbanks chose a hunting lodge, on Summit Drive above the Beverly Hills Hotel, and immediately brought in carpenters to expand it.

His optimism was rewarded when Pickford decided to brave the slings and arrows of public outrage and file for divorce, undaunted by her husband screaming that he would shoot that "climbing monkey"—referring to Doug, not Mary. So it was on March 28, 1920, Douglas Fairbanks and Mary Pickford, as the highlight of an intimate dinner party, were married in their new Beverly Hills home, which the press, not the newlyweds, took to calling Pickfair.

A sign once hung in Hollywood ordering *Dogs and Actors Keep Out.* The residents of Beverly Hills had felt the same way about actors, who were widely perceived as a shiftless, fly-by-night, just-a-notch-above-vagrant breed that you wouldn't want your sister, daughter, or ex-wife to marry. The entire film industry was considered shady. After all, it had come to Los Angeles to circumvent an Eastern patent-trust and to be near the Mexican border in case a quick getaway was necessary. Movie people were unquestionably a bad lot with loose morals.

As the industry grew, it became harder to dismiss all actors and their kind out of hand. By 1915 the payroll for the Los-Angeles-area movie business was already topping twenty million dollars a year. Stars were making ten thousand dollars a week and more in those days of tax-free income. Money has a way of creating respectability.

Because of geography, Beverly Hills would not be able to totally avoid movie people, but it could hope for the aristocracy of acting who had a modicum of social graces. Let the fast-talking sharpies stay in Hollywood where they belonged.

Divorced or not, Mary Pickford was someone to whom Beverly Hills could relate. She comported herself as a lady. As pioneer producer and later board chairman of Paramount Pictures, Adolph Zukor described her, "She was never extravagant, and she always appeared as she was, not as a big glamorous movie star .... She never cavorted with any boisterous society and was not a spendthrift or a wastrel."

To a degree, the town accepted Pickford and Fairbanks. The couple repaid the kindness by making Beverly Hills fashionable. Pickfair's guest list was extraordinary and enviable. The king and queen of Siam, Prince George of England, the crown prince of Japan, Charles Lindbergh, Babe Ruth, and Albert Einstein all came to dinner. One duke, duchess, and entourage of seventeen came for a weekend and stayed for months.

It didn't take long before more of the movie elite recognized the desirability of Beverly Hills. After all, if it was good enough for Doug and Mary, it must be pretty damn good. The city directory began to read like a list of the industry's top grossers.

Charlie Chaplin had a strangely shaped mansion built below Pickfair. Gloria Swanson lived above the hotel at 904 Crescent Drive. (Hers was one of the first homes in California with an elevator.) Rudolph Valentino moved into his Falcon's Lair. John Gilbert and Ina Claire shared a manor on Tower Road, as did King Vidor and Eleanor Boardman, and John Barrymore and Dolores Costello (although the latter's residence could be better described as a castle than a manor).

Universal Pictures founder Carl Laemmle had his Dias Dorados on Benedict Canyon. There was Tom Mix's 1010 Summit, Marion Davies's estate at 1700 Lexington Road, and Corinne Griffith's 912 Rexford Drive. Harold Lloyd had an enormous estate along Benedict Canyon on which his one hundred Great Danes ran free. At various times Greta Garbo lived in town as did Pauline Frederick, Richard Barthelmess, Wallace Beery, Walter Pidgeon, H. B. Warner, Ramon Navarro, Hunt Stromberg, Clara Bow, and Stan Laurel.

And best of all, there was Will Rogers, whose intervention managed to pry federal funds from Washington so that Beverly Hills could have its own post office.

"We're getting mail out here," he wrote to Andrew Mellon, secretary of the treasury, "and handling it in a tent. It's mostly circulars from Washington making speeches about prosperity and makes good reading while you are waiting for foreclosure. It seems you owe us $250,000 for a post office and they can't get the dough out of you. I told these folks I know you and that you wasn't that kind of a guy."

Mellon must not have been for the post office was built a short time later.

In 1920 Mrs. Anderson exercised her option to buy. By then the hotel was not only a profitable business venture, it was home. In 1919 her grandson, Robert, was born in Bungalow One. Son Stanley was taking over more and more of the nitty-gritty daily operations, leaving Mrs. Anderson the time and freedom to be the hotel's hostess.

Stanley Anderson was an active businessman with many interests. He owned a company that supplied the studios with cameras, was an investor in the original Fox Studios, and was a director of the corporation that built Westwood: today home of UCLA. He was shrewd enough to buy downtown Beverly Hills property early, and in his spare time was photographed with the likes of Charlie Chaplin and D. W. Griffith. Son Robert is under the impression that Stanley was part of the original Green group that planned Beverly Hills but pulled out when no one would go along with his idea for an English village motif.

In the twenties the hotel was considered a country retreat. In 1926, when the University of Southern California was facing a big football game against Notre Dame, the team went to the hotel to avoid fans. (It didn't help beat Knute Rockne's Fighting Irish. USC and its All-American back, Morton Kaer, lost by one point.) A local paper carried a picture of the team, trying to look nonchalant, in front of the hotel. What they looked was uncomfortable, probably because they were thirty to forty years younger than most of the other guests. If the coach was looking for a quiet, restful place, he found it. Some evenings the most exciting event was Mrs. Anderson rocking her rocking chair on the veranda.

Not that nothing ever happened. Once Stanley Anderson had to call police to break up a noisy poker game in the garage. A marshall was sent to investigate. After carefully assessing the situation, he took what seemed the best course of action. He anted up.

It is unknown if the marshall won any pots, but he definitely lost his job. An unamused city council replaced him by promoting the bicycle patrolman.

Then there were the feuding Chinese cooks in the kitchen, who from time to time took part in the ancient Chinese tradition of tong wars, and a sous-chef was handed the wrong end of a carving knife.

Except for such infrequent aberrations, Mrs. Anderson was successful in maintaining a dignified atmosphere. Flappers could go elsewhere. One did slip by, however, when Mrs. Anderson, in a show of goodwill, hosted a dinner for the community. The invitations clearly stated that formal attire was to be worn at dinner, which would be followed by a masked costume dance. One debutante, either an illiterate or a dyslexic, showed up a few minutes after everyone was seated in an outrageous pair of costume pajamas. The young woman had enough sense of propriety to be embarrassed.

The hotel was the site of most of the town's social events—dances, parties, and public recitals, which were often held in the lobby. Sometimes performers were local prodigies; at other times they were better-established and even prominent artists who were either town residents or hotel guests. Estelle Heartt Dreyfus, a contralto who performed at the opening of the Hollywood Bowl in 1922, gave a lobby recital when she was staying in one of the bungalows.

Sometimes a nonprofessional guest was prevailed upon to demonstrate an unusual talent. Miss Bathie Stuart, of New Zealand, rated a front-page story in the *Beverly Hills Citizen* when she performed Maori dances.

"Her costume was native, the skirt being of long strands of native flax decorated with herb juices so that it looked almost like beads. The bodice was of woven fibers, highly decorated. A feather cape was also worn. Her numbers included chants and songs in the Maori tongue and she gave a description of each and translated the words. The intonations and voice variations were remarkable and the music haunting."

Parties ranged from intimate affairs in the garden's round teahouse to galas in any of several larger rooms in the main building.

The teahouse was a beautiful little place that was usually arranged with a bandstand in the center and tables clustered around it. With doors thrown open on warm nights, and the intoxicating scents of hibiscus and camellias drifting in, the teahouse was a romantic and popular spot. Never open to the public, it was booked only for private parties, such as dinner dances, club meetings, and, in the case of Violette Johnson, a high tea.

To celebrate Violette's engagement to Fred Nason (owner of the Beverly Hills Moving and Transfer Company, a lucrative business in Southern California), she and her mother smothered the teahouse with violets of every shade of purple and held a tea for thirty.

There were several function rooms in the main building, with the Crystal Ballroom a favorite. This bilevel, pillared room was at the same time intimate and large. The red velvet and chandeliers gave it a charm and warmth not found in most hotel ballrooms.

Samuel Goldwyn would often rent the Crystal Room when he wanted to impress the world with his generosity and style. He threw a sumptuous party there when stars Vilma Banky and Rod La Rocque got married. As La Roque described it, "Sam just took over the hotel. There was a magnificent spread. Somebody says it was composed partly of papier-mache turkeys for display. The reception was so gargantuan, I guess the thought suggested itself. There was no papier-mache, believe me. It was certainly memorable. It was so funny—we thought we'd be married quietly in Santa Barbara."

In addition to being a party-center for the town—with only Pickfair as its rival—the hotel served as a community meeting place. On Sundays and Thursdays, the buffets were de rigueur because it was where everyone hobnobbed and because there weren't any other restaurants in town. The Beverly Hills Women's Club convened there until they built their own hall. (The club had originally been called the Beverly Hills Woman's Club, growing out of the woman's-rights movement of the late nineteenth century. In the twentieth century, members decided *woman's* was ungrammatical and changed the offending letter.)

Besides the women's club, the local realty board used the hotel facilities. On Sunday mornings, congregations without church buildings took over the ballrooms. In 1924 it was so congested that Episcopalians alternated Sundays with the Church of the Good Shepherd (which later earned the nickname of Our Lady of the Cadillacs).

The hotel also served as the center for local children's activities. One of the then-youngsters, Cecile Morrison, nee Woods, recalled a few years ago that the only recreation in Beverly Hills for anyone under eighteen was at the hotel. There was tennis, the pool, and, best of all, free movies. The hotel had the only public screening room in the area. You had to go all the way to Hollywood before you found another one. Everyone was invited to the films. Morrison and her sister, Helen, paid five cents each to take the Toonerville Trolley to the hotel. Most of the other children arrived in chauffeur-driven limousines. Woolworth heiress Barbara Hutton one-upped everyone by coming with a chauffeur *and* a bodyguard.

Holidays were special at the hotel. There were egg rolls on the lawn and entertainers like Jocko, the monkey. Christmases were the best times. In 1926 three trees on the lawn were decorated at a special ceremony with 175 colored lights. The next year an "ice palace" was built in the sunroom, and on Christmas Eve, a six-foot, eight-inch Santa Claus crawled out in time to light the tree and hear twenty choirboys from the Saint Thomas Church sing carols.

It is impossible to say if the hotel set the tone for the community or vice versa, but they were well-suited for each other. Beverly Hills in the early years was insular and self-contented without being "snobbish," as one observer, a longtime society reporter, put it. "It was their world, and that was sufficient."

It is not surprising then, that many residents were dismayed, some of them even outraged, when they learned in 1923 that Los Angeles was trying to annex their community.

At the time, Los Angeles was in an annexing frenzy. One small town after another was cajoled into becoming part of Los Angeles with the promise that it would be plugged into the city's water system.

Los Angeles had started out as a pueblo of 28 acres and ended up a megaloposis of 450 square miles. Will Rogers worried his home state of Oklahoma would be gobbled up next. While the Los Angeles sprawl never went far enough east to reach Tulsa, it soon completely surrounded Beverly Hills. It seemed natural, at least to the annexors, that Beverly Hills be their next annexee.

Beverly Hills already had a major problem on its hands. The Rodeo Land and Water Company had given notice that it wanted out. Supplying water to the town was no longer as profitable as it once had been, and the company was trying to renege on its contract.

Luckily for the town, it had recently hired a bright young city attorney, a graduate of the Harvard Law School, who had studied utilities law under Felix Frankfurter, later an associate justice of the Supreme Court.

The city attorney, Paul E. Schwab, believing there was a case against Rodeo Land and Water, sued.

It might have been a coincidence, but it was only after Beverly Hills sued that the annexation movement began. Schwab didn't believe in convenient coincidences. In fact, as was later noted, he believed that "the annexation question arose direcly from [the] suit. Apparently legal counsel of the utility company had advised its client to encourage the annexation as a way around court action; if Beverly Hills came under the jurisdiction of Los Angeles, the company would no longer be responsible for its water supply. The company accepted this advice and in a very short time collected enough signatures to force a special election on annexation."

The election was set for April 24, 1923. The days before were filled with door-to-door canvassing of Beverly Hills' one thousand registered voters. The pros argued "annexation or stagnation." The antis countered that the election was a cheap ploy by Los Angeles to get Beverly Hills' rich tax base. The Rodeo Land and Water Company hung an enormous pro-annexation sign at the the corner of Canon and Santa Monica.

On election morning, residents found bottles of putrid water on their doorsteps. An accompanying note said that town water would look like what was in the bottle if annexation did not go through.

The "noes" countered this dirty trick by staging a parade around Beverly Hills, with some of the town's most prominent residents marching—Will Rogers, director Fred Niblo, Douglas Fairbanks, Mary Pickford, Harold Lloyd, Conrad Nagel, Rudolph Valentino, and Tom Mix, among others. The stars offered free autographed pictures in exchange for votes against annexation.

In the end, Beverly Hills voted against losing its sovereignty to the promise of clean water. Annexation went down 507 to 337. Of course, in years to come, some people wondered who really won the war, since water in Beverly Hills became almost undrinkable, much to the delight of the bottled water companies.

And so the twenties passed.

The hotel enjoyed profit and success. It was already an institution—it doesn't take long for institutions and legends to be established in Southern California—and it seemed as if its success, like the nation's prosperity, was there to stay.

chapter four

The parties were bigger...the pace was faster...the shows were broader, the buildings were higher, the morals were lower and the liquor was cheaper.

F. SCOTT FITZGERALD
summing up the Roaring Twenties

The Roaring Twenties. The hurly-burly, Charleston-flapping, speculating, money-making Roaring Twenties. Some of it is the distortion of memory and those grainy newsreels, but people really thought the good times were there to stay.

Prosperity was as plain as the figures on the financial page and the Model A, with its gear-shift transmission, in the garage. The country's gross national product was rising and union membership dropping. (Who needed unions when wages had never been higher?) American goods were flooding the world, and new millionaires were being made all the time. (There were more millionaires—511—in 1929 than there were in the 1960s, when the population had risen by 50 percent.)

To some extent, this euphoria was induced by the stock market, which had become a national fad that could make anyone with the right tips and a little margin as rich as Rockefeller. *Get aboard* the speculation train, Hearst columnist Arthur Brisbane exhorted. People heeded his advice and scrambled on.

The fluctuations of the market were as much the talk of the town as Babe Ruth's batting average and the new movie at the Bijou. People ate, drank, and probably dreamed the market; so much so that when Charlie Chaplin mentioned his blood pressure had fallen, playwright George S. Kaufman immediately asked if it were common or preferred. The Marx Brothers were getting tips from elevator operators, chauffeurs from employers, nurses from patients. Between 1923 and 1929, the number of shares traded went from 236 million to 1.25 billion a year. Samuel Insull was able to parlay a gift from Thomas Edison of fifteen thousand dollars worth of stock into a utilities empire worth three billion dollars.

Oompah-pa was out. Jazz was in, and Zelda Fitzgerald became fond of the Plaza fountain. It was presto tempo and getting faster.

Madcap cavortings and challenging conventions were not to everyone's liking. Some people refused to raise their hemlines or lower their moral standards. Shocked or bemused, they watched from the sidelines and wondered where it would all end.

The Beverly Hills was steadfastly not a Jazz Age hotel, as hurly-burly was not Mrs. Anderson's style. Here rooms, suites, and bungalows were sanctuaries from the excesses of the era and were filled to capacity by people, like Cornelius Vanderbilt, Jr., who wished to escape the antics occurring elsewhere. Although some people sniffed that the Beverly

Hills was little better than a retirement home, its accountants had no cause for complaint.

There were other places for the hooch set, anyway. One was the infamous Garden of Allah, which opened January 9, 1927. Its owner was the exotic-eyed Russian-born screen star Alla Nazimova, who having free-spent her way through a fortune, turned her West Hollywood mansion into a hotel. From its opening, the Garden of Allah had the reputation of being a place where the movie industry went to carry on, a place for mistresses and affairs, not wives and weddings. One producer called it "a glorified whorehouse."

Twenty-five thin-walled villas—anything and everything could be heard from adjoining rooms—were tucked around an enormous pool, which was the scene of countless parties and dunkings. Tallulah Bankhead, a lady whose reputation had a lot in common with the Garden's—she was known to give interviews perched on a grand piano so that the reporter couldn't help noticing her lack of underwear—was one of the guests. One night she dove into the pool in full evening regalia, diamonds and all. Bankhead was not a good swimmer to begin with and was made less so by the long dress. To keep from drowning, Bankhead peeled it off, yelling, "Everybody's been dying to see my body. Now they can see it."

Even without the encumbrance of the dress, it didn't appear that Bankhead was going to make it out of the pool. Johnny Weissmuller, in the best tradition of Tarzan, dove in and rescued her.

There was always something going on at the Garden—though usually not something you'd write home to mother about. Even an innocent, early-morning stroll could mean being accosted by humorist Robert Benchley, once described as someone who "never seemed quite drunk, but was usually a little pixilated." Benchley would invite anyone passing by to join him for a drink—and another and another—no matter the time of day. He stayed at the Garden whenever he was in town without his wife; otherwise, he stayed at the Beverly Hills.

If the Garden was too wild and the Beverly Hills too tame, after December 1927, people could go to the Beverly Wilshire, a large downtown hotel modeled after a Florentine palazzo. It was nine stories high, had three hundred and fifty rooms and apartments, six ballrooms, and space for eight shops. Reports had it costing three million dollars to build, and it was touted as the last word in apartment-hotels.

Mrs. Anderson attended the opening night party there and brought some of her own guests with her. With her usual graciousness, she wished the Wilshire's owner, builder Walter G. McCarty, every success, and he thanked her for "the kindly motive that prompts your congratulations," as the photographers' flashbulbs popped.

Mrs. Anderson could afford to be gracious. She had a long and loyal guest list. In this time of prosperity, there were enough guests to fill all the hotels.

The Hills did lose some of its party and event business to the Wilshire. The annual Chamber of Commerce dinner, which earned many column-inches of publicity for having guests of honor like Mary Pickford and Jack Benny, alternated between the two establishments. (It was at one of those dinners that Benny received the title of Honorary Dogcatcher of Beverly Hills. Reportedly he was somewhat peeved that he hadn't been given the same title that Will Rogers had received, that of honorary mayor. Benny should have realized that in Beverly Hills, no one was in Rogers's league. Edgar Bergen introduced his newest sidekick, Mortimer Snerd, at one of the dinners, as well.)

While there were those who sought the novelty and newness of the Wilshire, others remained faithful to the Hills, especially to the Crystal Room. Mr. and Mrs. Basil

Rathbone threw a small costume party for four hundred there.

The good times at the Hills were about to end, but not because of its competition. It was to fall victim to the economic time bombs and excesses that would soon blast the entire country apart.

The Hills might have been able to ride out the maelstrom except for one thing. By the time the stock market crashed in October 1929, Mrs. Margaret Anderson no longer owned the Beverly Hills Hotel. She had sold out in November 1928.

Nineteen twenty-eight was a seller's year. People had money to spare and money to invest. There was a frantic scramble for properties. As happened fifty years later, in the 1980s, it didn't matter if the buyer had any familiarity with a business. There was some misguided perception that if you could manage one business, you could manage another, that selling buttons was the same as selling books. The buying, the *acquiring*, was the thing. Helena Rubenstein sold her cosmetics company for $7.5 million—she was able to buy it back one year after the crash for $1 million.

At least the purchaser of the Hills, Hugh Leighten, had some knowledge of hotelkeeping. His Chicago-based company, Interstate, owned a resort-lodge in the High Sierras. Leighten paid $1.5 million for the Beverly Hills, half of which he raised by going public with 6 1/2-percent-interest bonds.

Interstate took over in December 1928 and immediately changes were made. Serving as his own general manager for the first few months, Leighten tried to get rid of the hotel's retirement home image. He saw a younger crowd spending big money at the Wilshire, and he wanted to capture some of that wealth.

Subtlety was not Leighten's strong suit. If he wanted the Hills to kick up its heels and become part of the flapper era, he wanted the world to know about it—and fast. Rob Wagner, a humorist with a magazine called the *Beverly Hills Script* ("The Swindling Servants of the Film Stars! Our Low Aims, also Comment—Gossip—Fiction—News—Society—Business—Gags—Reviews") wrote this four months after Leighten took over the hotel:

"The center of social life was the Beverly Hills Hotel, which became a quiet harbor into which old and old-fashioned people of wealth withdrew. Jazz descended upon the world, but that grand old pile remained untouched by its flamboyancies. It seemed that the Beverly Hills Hotel was to take its place with the historic institutions of the country.

"Then, almost overnight, it changed its character. Where once the ancient hostelry lay hidden behind its sheltering pines and palms, it has suddenly burst forth at night in carnival splendor, its facade ablaze with a battery of red, yellow and blue squirt-lights suggesting nothing so much as Queen Victoria turned Follies girl, wearing a blonde wig and doing a toe dance in pink tights.

"... the whole character of the hotel is undergoing a change. Additions and fresh decorations are underway, tennis and dancing are part of its new life and everywhere there is evidence that its drift toward what the youngsters called an old ladies' home has suddenly been arrested ...henceforth it will hold up its head with the Beverly Wilshire Hotel and the competing joyousness of the Hollywood centers of social interest. Shocking at first to us old timers, we realize that this startling rejuvenation of our beloved hostelry is but one evidence of a change that has been gradually creeping over our entire city, now made so dramatically apparent."

The real shocks and changes were still waiting offstage and would not be caused by a few red, yellow, and blue lights. Leighten went blithely ahead with his alterations, as he and most of his fellow citizens were blissfully unaware that the bottom was about to fall out. The handwriting had been on the wall for sometime, but no one likes to read bad news. There were a few who warned of the approaching cataclysm, but they couldn't be heard over the popping of champagne corks.

Herbert Hoover, for one, sounded an alarm as early as January 1926. "There are some phases of the situation which requires caution...real estate and stock speculation and its possible extension into commodities with inevitable inflation .... This fever of speculation...can only land us on the shores of overdepression."

In Leighten's defense, it should be noted that the purchase of the Beverly Hills, with its sixteen acres in a rapidly growing, prosperous community, was not crazy speculation. But to paraphrase the old real-estate adage, it was a question of timing, timing, timing. Leighten had the misfortune of buying and trying to change the hotel's image at the wrong time. He was then caught up in losing former clientele who disliked the change and being unable to find new guests because of the economy.

He hoped that with a stiff transfusion of money, he could make the Beverly Hills attractive to the freer-spending, younger crowd. Leighten intended to completely refurbish and redecorate. People's tastes had changed since the Beverly Hills was built. They wanted bigger rooms, more suites, and more bathrooms. The bungalows had been built that way, but many walls now needed to be knocked out in the main building. A new tennis clubhouse was needed, and there were also plans to change the children's dining room, as well as add to the shopping arcade.

To better concentrate on the facelift, Leighten turned over the general managership to Leon Brooks, who was fresh from the Alexander Young Hotel in Honolulu. Leighten needed more than extra time to realize his alteration plans. He needed money. Once the stock market swan-dived, money was hard to come by.

The carnage on Wall Street not only wiped out investors, speculators, and dabblers, it destroyed the confidence of the nation. People wanted to hold on to their money for the worst that they feared was yet to come. They weren't about to risk investing in rugs and furnishings for a hotel in Southern California. Hoarding started on a large scale. People with money withdrew it from banks and deposited it out of the country or into their mattresses.

Six months after Black Friday, the *New York Times* reported the obvious. Americans weren't buying cars, clothes, or other consumer items. They were running scared and holding onto their money in those rainy times that were building to hurricane force. As more businesses went under and defaulted on bank loans, investment money became scarcer.

The Beverly Hills Hotel, for the first time in its history, was losing money. The longtime guests who had stuck around were spending less on room service and meals—hotel operations that make the difference between profit and loss. The free-spending guests Leighten had been seeking, didn't leave the Wilshire. The only glamour types to check in at the Beverly Hills were those seeking seclusion.

In 1932, when Greta Garbo wanted to be more alone than usual, she took up residence in a bungalow, confident she would be well out of the Hollywood social scene. And to doubly ensure that she wouldn't be bothered, she took all her meals in her room.

She pretty much got her wish for solitude except for the time word of her whereabouts reached some particularly persistent fans. They had camped out in the lobby hoping for a glimpse of the Swedish actress. For a time their doggedness went unrewarded. Garbo remained a whispered-about presence that never materialized. One afternoon, one of the whispers mentioned a car coming up the driveway in preparation for a quick escape.

Garbo was already in the backseat of the beat-up Packard, and the car was pulling away down the driveway, when the fans scrambled out the front door. It looked as if Garbo had outflanked them again. One tenacious fan would not give up. She ran after the car, jumped onto the hood, and flattened her face against the windshield, getting a precious peek at her elusive prey.

Clark Gable was another star who used the Hills as a hideaway. He did so when he separated from his wife Ria. There was an uproar in the press and among his fans. Of course, his choice of hotels resulted in more fodder for the the gossip mills, as the word went out that he was using his bungalow for assignations with *Call of the Wild* co-star, Loretta Young. When Young temporarily cancelled out of her next movie, *Ramona*, it was rumored she was pregnant with Gable's baby.

Gable also used the hotel during his affair with Carole Lombard. As Lombard told Garson Kanin, "We used to go through the God-damnest routine you ever heard of. He'd get somebody to go hire a room or bungalow somewhere. Like on the outskirts. A couple of times at the Beverly Hills Hotel...Then the somebody would give him a key, then he'd have another key made and give it to me. Then we'd arrange a time and he'd get there. Then I'd get there....Then with all the shades down and all the doors and windows locked and the phones shut off, we'd have a drink or sometimes not. He's not much of a bottle man. And we'd get going. And that's how it went for quite some time."

Guests like Gable and Garbo who stay at a hotel so as not to attract attention generally don't. The Hills was not getting guests who drew other guests. In the twenties, the Mary Pickfords went to the hotel because they liked associating with the old-money, patrician guests. In a snowball effect, the fact that Mary Pickford went to the Hills attracted other movie-folk who wanted some of her respectability to rub off on them. By the early thirties, the hotel had lost its magnetism, and it was in deep trouble.

Leighten brought in one manager after another; none could turn the hotel around. In 1931 he hired W. M. Kimball, a man with wide and varied hotel experience, including former ownership of the Hotel Springfield in Springfield, Massachusetts. Still the ledger got redder and redder.

In 1933 the crisis was reached.

The nation was singing the "Starvation Blues." Foreclosures were averaging a thousand a day, and one out of every five children wasn't getting enough to eat. On March 4, Franklin Delano Roosevelt was sworn in as our thirty-second president, saying it was "time to speak the truth, the whole truth, frankly and boldly. Nor need we shrink from honestly facing conditions in our country today. This great nation will endure as it has endured, will revive and prosper. So...let me assert my firm belief that the only thing to fear is fear itself."

Interstate, honestly facing conditions at the hotel, decided it could no longer pump money into the failing enterprise at the rate it had been. In addition to the onerous operating deficits, there were still $731,000 in outstanding bonds on which the 6 1/2-percent interest had to be paid.

Interstate tried striking a compromise with the bond-holders. It offered to pay 2 percent interest for five years and 4 1/2 percent for the following five years. Any profit made in the first five-year period would be put into a sinking fund to help pay the later higher rate.

Unfortunately, many of the bondholders could not be contacted in time for the compromise to be okayed. And those that were, were not overjoyed with the offer.

Consequently, on Friday, April 14, 1933, Interstate announced it would put no more money into the hotel. The Beverly Hills would close, effective immediately.

Luckily for the remaining guests, manager Kimball interceded. As he explained it to the *Beverly Hills Citizen*, "The original order was to close at once but on account of many elderly people in the bungalows, I succeeded in deferring the closing until the guests had the opportunity to make arrangements for their care."

In relation to what was happening in the United States, putting one hundred comparatively well off, albeit elderly, people on the street in 1933 was not of tremendous consequence. Just one year before, 273,000 people were evicted when their homes were foreclosed. According to historian Caroline Bird, one-fourth of the entire state of Mississippi was auctioned off at a foreclosure sale in a single day.

This was a time when urban families moved every two or three months, skipping out in the middle of the night to avoid paying past-due rents. One Philadelphia moving company owner got his start by specializing in middle-of-the-night jobs. He had families packed up and out by dawn, just in time to beat the sheriff's sale. Bird saw this period as having "more far-reaching consequences...than either of the World Wars. Nobody escaped. Every individual in every walk of life was hit."

Putting those one hundred people on the streets in Beverly Hills was striking proof that no one and nothing was safe from the Depression.

Residents of Beverly Hills were stunned. The hotel had been so much a part of the community for so long that everyone assumed it would endure. The city itself had escaped many of the hardships of the Depression primarily because the entertainment industry was one that prospered in hard times. People needed something to make them forget their troubles, if only for ninety minutes, and Myrna

Loy slinking around in satin outfits was the very thing. It didn't matter how down and out you were, somehow you managed to find the dime, deep in your pocket, for the price of a movie ticket.

On April 19, five days after the first announcement, the hotel closed its doors, and the one-hundred-member staff was let go. Except for a few bungalow tenants, it was completely empty—no gardeners, no caretakers, not even security guards, no one.

Carolyn Talbot Hoagland was one of the tenants. "Vacant, the large rambling hotel resembled a haunted house. Perhaps the tennis courts were kept up. I don't remember a pool, at least not one filled with water....That year [1933] my father had a temporary position in Los Angeles. My mother, my younger sister and I moved from Ohio to live with him in one of the bungalows. For a starstruck teen-ager, the best of all was the fact that in a bungalow two doors away lived a movie star, Gene Raymond."

The bondholders were quick to realize that whatever value was left on their investment would be lost if the hotel was not maintained. They might be able to recoup *something* if there was anything left worth selling. With that in mind, a bondholders' protective committee was formed in May to determine what should become of the hotel. The committee consisted of Robert J. Giles, a vice-president of the Occidental Life Insurance Company; Ralph Reed, an architect; and Ernest U. Schroeter, a lawyer who also acted as counsel for the committee.

The committee's first action was to appeal to other bondholders to place their securities with the Bank of America, which would act as a depository. Once enough of them had done so, the committee, with the help of the bank, would start foreclosure proceedings. The committee made it clear, however, that it would have to receive a satisfactory bid. If it didn't, bondholders would take title to the hotel and "either sell or lease it by the opening of the fall season."

In all likelihood, anyone with a ten-thousand-dollar-cash down payment could have walked away with the hotel, but no one with the cash made an offer. In spite of the committee's declaration, the hotel did not open in the fall.

In December, the committee had its first piece of good news for the bondholders. It had found a lessee in Frank E. Dimmick, described by the *Los Angeles Times* as a "nationally known hotel man."

Dimmick took a long-term lease for five hundred thousand dollars and reopened in early 1934. In a sense, he was opening a new hotel, having little cachet of goodwill to fall back on. He would have to establish a reputation. Dimmick had all of Leighten's problems and then some. Besides having to find new guests, he had to hire and train a new staff. The one advantage he had over his predecessor, and not one to be discounted, was his ability to raise money for renovations and redecoration—not enough for everything, but enough to get started.

By this time, the hotel was bordering on shabby and needed a tremendous amount of work. Dimmick began modestly, adding bathrooms, enlarging a few rooms, and what was to prove to be the most propitious alteration—coverting the children's dining room into a dark, cozy cocktail lounge.

Prohibition had had a devastating effect on many restaurants and hotels. Very often the success of such operations depends on liquor sales, not on food and rooms. During the life of the Volstead Act, many hotels went under, including some of New York City's most fashionable: the Knickerbocker, the Buckingham, the Manhattan. The Beverly Hills had been largely unaffected by the

Eighteenth Amendment because its success had never been based on receipts from a heavy-drinking crowd.

With that history, it's ironic that the new bar was soon the most profitable part of Dimmick's operation. It became a hangout, a den of drinking for Hollywood's original Rat Pack, an Algonquin West, minus the Roundtable. This hard-boozing group of cynics included W. C. Fields; John Barrymore; writer and journalist Gene Fowler; painter John Decker; humorist Wilson Mizner; eccentric artist Sadakichi Hartmann; and cartoonist George McManus, with occasional appearances by Will Rogers, producer Darryl Zanuck and his polo-playing chums.

A manic bunch of nihilists, they would not have been allowed into the hotel by Mrs. Anderson (who died in 1930); but on the other hand, they wouldn't have wanted to be. When they descended on the bar, which was originally called the Jardin, they took over the place, trying diligently to follow Field's dictum that "since the conundrum of life is so hard, the answer to it must be hard liquor."

As they soaked up the booze, it was their habit and plea- sure to cast jaundiced eyes on the pretensions and absurdi- ties of Hollywood and on themselves. Will Rogers once chided Barrymore with "Listen, Great Profile, there's many a Barrymore in the sticks behind long whiskers."

One long-running discussion was an "I'll top you" on who had suffered more in younger, leaner days. Barrymore scored big with his story of poverty as a struggling cartoonist in San Francisco before the 1906 earthquake.

"My roommate and I were so hard up that the only asset we had between us was a fancy gold bridge in his mouth. When we were strapped, I yanked it out and slapped it in hock. The pawnbroker ate with it more frequently than my roommate, and on better fare. But when we had his bridge- work, we set up a slick routine for breakfast. He would order pancakes and coffee, eat half the portion, and then, with neat timing, I would dash into the restaurant waving a fake telegram. He'd seize the wire and spring off frantically with it. I would stare after him dolefully, then sit down and finish his pancakes and coffee."

The group, even when sober, was unpredictable, but after a session at the Jardin, it was best to hide your women and children, or in Mrs. Will Rogers's case, the stemware. One evening, having spent a good deal of time in the bar, W. C. Fields thought he might drop in on Rogers, with whom he had worked in the Ziegfeld Follies. Rogers and Mrs. Rogers were staying at the hotel, as was Fields. Earlier in the day, Mrs. Rogers had purchased a set of very expensive—and very fragile—crystal goblets in one of the hotel's shops. She had them sitting out on a table when Fields came to call. Spotting them, Fields took a swig from a cocktail shaker he carried for emergencies, grabbed the glasses, and proceeded to juggle them at dizzying speed. It's unclear if Mrs. Rogers remembered that Fields had been consummate juggler in his vaudevillian days. What is known is that she did not think highly of the impromptu performance. Once she was able to extricate the glasses from his grasp, she had her husband escort Fields back to his own room.

These habitues of the Jardin took their drinking and playing seriously and were seriously put out when merrymaking was denied them. George McManus, the creator of "Maggie and Jiggs," came into the bar one night very much out of sorts. He had been denied admittance—not having been invited—to some big, exclusive bash being held in the hotel. As he drank more, he became incensed and determined to crash the party. Finally he came up with a solution. McManus hurried into the men's room, removed the *PRESS* button from a urinal, and gained entrance as a member of the Fourth Estate. The Three Stooges later wrote this into one of their movies.

The group had such a reputation for being insane and bizarre that people easily believed the legend that arose after Barrymore's death. Supposedly the pack stole his body from the funeral parlor, propped it up in his favorite chair, and proceeded to have a party in his honor. According to the story, they forgot to tell Errol Flynn about the guest of honor, and he almost fainted when he walked in to face what he thought was Barrymore returned from the dead.

Even with this crew's valiant efforts, the bar receipts weren't enough to save Dimmick's venture. Nor was the tennis crowd, which had made the Beverly Hills' courts *the* place to play. Pro Harvey Snodgrass gathered a fiercely loyal and very fashionable coterie of players including Gloria Swanson, Mrs. Ernst Lubitsch, David O. Selznick, and Mrs. Sam Jaffe. (Years later, when Snodgrass retired to Arizona, he was unable to give up teaching. He was so good that he was able to sit in a chair on the court and hit the balls back to his pupils without getting up.)

By October 1936, the bondholders' committee met again for foreclosure discussions. By this time the Bank of America was no longer happy to be handling this pink elephant on Sunset Boulevard. The bank wanted to end its involvement as quickly as possible. It assigned the task to one of its brightest young men—an up-and-comer who was going to go far in the banking business. This fellow had already risen incredibly quickly through the Bank of America's ranks. He would certainly find a way to put the hotel back on its feet or, failing that, to find a buyer.

The bright young man was Hernando Courtright, and Hernando Courtright was about to bring his own version of the New Deal to the Beverly Hills Hotel.

chapter five

Sometimes life imitates the movies. At this point the history of the Beverly Hills Hotel begins to play like an episode of the Perils of Pauline.

Hotel in distress. Bulldozers in the ready. A knight in shining armor (preferably one who knows credits from debits) to come swooping in and snatch the hotel from the jaws of destruction.

Strike that.

In keeping with the Southern California locale, make it a dashing caballero, a Zorro, charging in and taking command. Call Central Casting for someone imaginative, handsome, and able to pull managerial and money miracles from beneath his cloak.

Actually, forget Central Casting and put the call through to Bank of America. Hernando Courtright was made for the role. He was all the above, plus he had a background that would made any studio press agent weep with joy.

You want dashing caballero? Courtright's Basque-born mother was a descendant of the Aztec-conquering Spanish explorer Hernando Cortez. There was a Hernando in the family in every succeeding generation.

Want romance, adventure? Mama Courtright met Papa Courtright when he, an Irish-American cavalry officer, was stationed at the U. S. embassy in Mexico City.

After the wedding, they moved to Coeur D'Alene, Idaho, (admittedly, straying from the exotic storyline) not to mine lead and silver which had been discovered there in 1882, but to ranch cattle.

Now comes the pathos. It turned out Papa Courtright was not much of a rancher. "Father knew a lot about horses, but not much about cattle."

Hernando was a strong-willed child who chose a spanking over obeying an order to pick berries on his eighth birthday. He also chose not to follow in his father's footsteps but instead to heed the advice of Irish Grandmother Kelley—the main thing, she said, is to go out and make money.

Courtright earned his first degree from the University of California, Berkeley. His second came from the University of Southern California's School of Business, where in the good company of Fred Nason (remember Violette and the teahouse engagement party?) and Howard Ahmanson, Sr. (founder and chairman of the Home Savings & Loan Association), Courtright was named Least Likely to Succeed.

With his business degree in hand, Courtright took a job with the "People's Bank," otherwise known as the Bank of America, at its headquarters in San Francisco.

The B of A's story is one of quintessential American grit and luck. It was founded in 1904 as the Bank of Italy when A. P. Giannini became annoyed with conventional bank policies of the day. He felt the "little man," the small depositor, was being shortchanged. Banks weren't interested in the little guy, but Giannini was, so he set up his own financial institution. His bank enjoyed only modest success until the morning of the San Francisco earthquake.

It was 5:13 a.m., on Wednesday, April 18, 1906, when San Francisco was shaken to its foundations for twenty-eight seconds. Sidewalks buckled. Streets cracked. Chimneys fell. Crudely built buildings crumbled. The horrific devastation came from fires that flared up all over the city. Fire trucks raced frantically throughout the city with no organization or orchestration and very little effect. Soon blazes were raging out of control. San Francisco looked as if it were burning out of existence.

That afternoon, Giannini thought it best to abandon his building in the financial district and transport the bank's gold and records to safer, less flammable areas.

His foresight paid off nine days later. Other banks were still in chaos and gridlock, sifting through smoldering and charred records and waiting for vaults to cool enough to be unlocked. Giannini had his records intact and his money ready to dispense. The Bank of Italy was back in business. He set about handing out Rebuild San Francisco loans from the bank's new headquarters—a plank laid across two barrels.

The Bank of America, nee the Bank of Italy, was on its way to becoming one of the largest financial concerns in the world.

Some thirty years later, Courtright brought a knack for making money to the Bank of America, a knack which helps an ambitious young man get ahead in banking. Within a short time, Courtright was promoted to vice-president and transferred to Los Angeles. His duties there were varied, and for no particular reason, he was assigned the Beverly Hills Hotel, "to occupy my time."

The bank still held the $731,000 worth of bonds, which in January 1937 the bondholder's committee bought for $320,000 at a foreclosure sale. Courtright was the bank's representative on the committee. The bonds were purchased to give the committee more flexibility in handling the hotel's affairs and also to push out Dimmick, the leaseholder. E. J. Caldwell was brought over from the Hotel Roosevelt in Hollywood as the new manager. He had previously worked at the Edgewater Beach Hotel in Chicago, the Kapler chain in St. Louis, and various other smaller hotels in California.

When first given the assignment, Courtright's charge had been to either sell or save the hotel. When the committee still owned the hotel following the foreclosure sale, saving it was the only alternative.

Even with the new manager, Courtright found himself increasingly involved in hotel affairs.

"I used to get the department heads together and hold meetings in the evening after my banking duties were supposed to be over. At those meetings we asked ourselves 'Where is the money coming from to make a hotel a going concern?' We knew there was no money in a few elderly ladies sitting around the lobby.

"Then we asked ourselves, 'Who spends the money spent in a hotel?' The answer was simple: the businessman on an expense account. Little Miss Jones, left a small patrimony by her uncle, sits on her nest egg, but to an executive trying to close a deal for Consolidate or Vultee or Texaco, or to sign Bob Hope or Bing Crosby for a radio deal or an author imported by MGM to write a screenplay, an extra fifty bucks or so is a minor item. So, we decided to mix the carriage trade-resort business with a transient business to give us some constancy of income."

For someone new to hotelkeeping, Courtright showed a remarkable acumen for the business. Although his approach was not that of Mrs. Anderson's, she would have approved. Times had changed. If the hotel was to survive and prosper, it would have to change as well. Besides, Courtright was no Leighten, bringing in garish squirt-lights to gussy up and cheapen the place.

It was Courtright's intent to maintain the friendly, home-like atmosphere, but add to it so that the money-losing duckling could be transformed into a profit-making swan. To do that, in the words of *Los Angeles Times* columnist Jack Smith, Courtright would have to "wean out the age of lavender and lace."

The first priority became redecorating. Dimmick had begun, but now it was to proceed full steam ahead, at a cost of three thousand dollars per room. There was to be no Holiday Inn monotony. Each room would be different, done by some of the most famous and fashionable decorators of the day—Paul Lazlo, Jack Lucareni, Don Loper, Harriet Shellenberger.

It was Loper who came up with the most lasting and memorable touch—the distinctive pink and green banana-leaf wallpaper. The fronds are actually cut out and pasted onto the white walls. The design became so popular that women who wanted to copy it in their homes were tearing pieces of it off the ladies' room wall. After making several replacements, the management, in desperation, hung a sign reading *IF YOU REALLY WANT THIS, PLEASE CONTACT OUR DECORATOR.*

During the makeover, rooms and suites that hadn't been occupied in years were discovered. In the lobby, nonfunctional pillars were moved to make the area lighter and airier. Remaining untouched was the constantly lit hearth, which must have appealed to Courtright's Spanish heritage. The fire, which burned twenty-four hours a day, first with wood and later gas, was a symbol of the old Spanish-mission hospitality. In the early days, missions were built a day's journey apart so that travelers would always find a warm fire and a glass of wine at the end of the wearying day's trek. In another acknowledgment of the past, Courtright had a chain-of-ownership map of Rodeo de las Aguas hung in the hotel's front office.

The gardens, much of which had gone to weed, had to be replanted. At some point, Courtright had the now-famous Brazilian pepper tree planted in the cocktail lounge's courtyard. When the tree started ailing, he had a smaller one planted on the other side of the fence for cross-pollination, thereby saving the original.

At the lower level, near the coffee shop, a new shopping arcade was built. It was there that Francis Taylor opened his art gallery. Although in art circles he was famous in his own right, to the rest of the world he would be known best as Elizabeth's father. The young starlet began her long association with the hotel when she visited his gallery and occasionally posed for publicity stills there. ("Frances Taylor's art gallery...where daughter Elizabeth, young M-G-M actress, helps him dress the window for an exhibit.") For a time there was also a dance studio—Miss O'Kane's Dancing School—in the arcade, near the door to the pool. The Miss O'Kane was Eileen O'Kane Fegtex, wife of set designer Ernst Fegtex.

As much time as Courtright gave the hotel, it wasn't enough. He was finding that certain functions couldn't be delegated and creating an image was one of them. It took a special perspective and personality, which Courtright possessed. He was spending less time at the bank and more at the Hills.

He was drawn to the hotel while people were drawn to him. And why not? Courtright was a handsome, outgoing man, who could best be described as charming. Years later, someone was to say that he was "probably the best-liked man in Southern California. I don't think Hernando has a serious enemy anywhere, with the possible exception of Ben Silberstein." (More on Ben L. Silberstein later.)

They talk about "naturals" in sports, someone who has an inborn sense of the game. Courtright was a natural to hotelkeeping. Before receiving the Beverly Hills file, he had

had no hotel experience other than having stayed at several and knowing what he liked about them. But from somewhere within came this intuitiveness about what would work and what wouldn't, what it took to make guests feel welcome and eager to return.

Take the name of the cocktail lounge. The Jardin. The Garden. There was a small garden outside on the patio and the many acres of hotel grounds were one enormous garden, yet the name didn't work. It was unevocative and unmemorable. When a new name suggested itself, Courtright went with it. That name—the Polo Lounge.

Polo was introduced to the West Coast in 1882 by Horace A. Vachell, a British settler and novelist. Poor Mr. Vachell was the subject of endless ribbing about his strange behavior on the ponies and his even stranger choice of game attire.

"Hey, Horus," he was asked, "why do you wear your drawers outside your pants?"

Polo got past its rocky beginning and by the 1920s had become *the* sport to play. Among its aficionados were 20th Century-Fox's Darryl F. Zanuck, the ubiquitous Will Rogers, Tommy Hitchcock—one of the greats of the sport—Robert Stack, and Spencer Tracy. One of the polo players, Deering Davis, became director of decor at the Hills in the 1960s. He remembered that Will Rogers's polo field was "on the top of the hill overlooking the Riviera Country Club. We would stop here at the hotel for a drink on the way to Santa Barbara, or to Midwick in Pasadena, where the good, high-goal polo was played. A lot of movie people were attracted to polo. Jack Holt [a star of numerous action films including *Holt of the Secret Service*] was one of the early enthusiasts. [*Our Gang* producer] Hal Roach was a good player, and Will Rogers was a bad player but a helluva hot enthusiast. He was the world's worst sport. He hated to lose, and he showed it. Darryl Zanuck played, but not very well. He had a good team around him."

It's widely believed that the Polo Lounge was so named because these players frequented it, but according to Courtright, who should have known, that wasn't the case. By his recollection, the name evolved from a favor for a friend, Charles Wrightsman. Wrightsman had a polo team that won the national championship. On receiving the championship silver bowl, he fretted over where to keep it. Since it was a team effort, it didn't seem right to keep it on a shelf in his home. When Wrightsman mentioned this quandry, Courtright offered to display the bowl in the bar, which was being redecorated anyway. From the favor came the name.

As any good banker would hope, Courtright's efforts were paying off. A small profit of $17,335.25 was realized in the first quarter after Dimmick had been pushed out by the bondholders' committee. The success wasn't completely due to Courtright's efforts. Unlike Leighten who bought the hotel at terrible time, the Bank of America executive became involved at a propitious one.

The Depression was ending and the bitter residue that remained would be washed away by the war effort. People were traveling again and spending money to make money again. Businessmen were on the move, and the Beverly Hills was getting the word out that it could make their trips more pleasant and even fun.

Part of that fun came from Charlie Chaplin having lunch at his table, Table 1, in the Polo Lounge. (It was the only table with an exclusive reservation. If Chaplin did not show, no one else was allowed to sit there.) It was being able to squint through the darkness at Errol Flynn imbibing with playboy Freddie McAvoy, who usually had his butler George in tow. George's primary function was to keep Freddie's tumbler filled with Russian vodka. And it was probably fun, once the shock wore off, to witness Captain Horace Brown, a William Randolph Hearst lookalike whom Marion Davies later married, test-driving his new trail bike—through the Polo Lounge. (He managed to test drive it out before anyone had the presence of mind to stop him.)

The hotel's registry was showing the names of America's corporate elite, company presidents, oilmen, and bankers. They were attracted to the Hills more for its atmosphere than its accommodations. It was heady stuff sharing air space with countesses, duchesses, and movie queens. The chairman of the National City Bank of New York liked telling his country club pals back home that he checked in behind the Prince and Princess of Tchokotck, who were in Beverly Hills on a shopping excursion. The retired president of Socony Vacuum got a kick having a drink next to the Baroness de Kuffner, whose name always appeared on the best-dressed lists of Paris.

Habitues of the hotel ranged from Katharine Hepburn to Countess "Babs" Bonet Willaumez. (Hepburn was an avid tennis player. She would show up at the courts with her sheepdog. The well-trained pet would sit on the then-vacant lot across what the locals call "The Alley," but on the map shows up as Glen Way. One of the most repeated stories about the hotel concerns the time, following a very strenuous and hot set, Hepburn went from the courts to the pool and dove in fully clothed. The lady was in a hurry to cool off.)

Hills parties were once again "A" parties, the "must" ones to which you had to be invited or face social ostracism. In attendance at a cocktail party thrown for Countess Willaumez, something of a fashion dignitary, were Constance and Joan Bennett, Gilbert Roland, the David Selznicks, Cary Grant, Miriam Hopkins, and Mrs. Jules Stein. (Stein was the founder of MCA. An ophthalmologist, he gave up eye-doctoring to start an agency for musicians playing in speakeasies. MCA went on to become an entertainment giant.)

Ouida Bergere Rathbone was a social butterfly who favored the Hills. Born Ida Berger, she had been head of Paramount Pictures' script department before making her best career move by marrying Basil Rathbone. She then devoted her energies to giving parties. One was an extravagant charity ball in 1939. *Time*, with the cattiness that was its trademark then, gave the affair the following write-up:

"The project was sumptuous. Piece de resistance was to have been an Alpine scene re-created with real snow in the sub-tropical palm gardens of the Beverly Hills Hotel. Afternoon of the party the rains came. What with this disappointment and that, by 7 in the evening Mrs. Rathbone was in a state of nervous collapse and could not take part in the festivities. But her guests had a high old time inside the big, rambling hotel where only the jollification was wet.

"Everybody was just getting happily awash when the Beverly Hills police arrived to break up the crap game. The more prudish producers went home. By 2 o'clock only the drunks and the pretty girls were left. At 4 the fights began. By 6 the flunkeys were mopping up and sweeping together the fragments. Next day people counted their hang-overs, declared it was one of the best Hollywood parties ever. There was some question whether the party made any money. After the 1938 party the charity was reported to be only $2,000 in the red."

More typical of the events at the hotel was the party Edgar Bergen threw for his dummy, Charlie McCarthy, after they had finished making *You Can't Cheat An Honest Man*. Even *Life* went to that party—no wonder poor Candice Bergen felt that McCarthy was a sibling with whom she was competing. Two hundred of Hollywood's finest turned out to find the ballroom converted into an old-time music hall, with a row of penny-arcade stereoscopes at one end showing *Little Egypt* and *The Great Train Robbery.*

The seven-year-old son of a popular nightclub entertainer had his birthday party at the hotel at the end of the thirties. The entertainer, who was such a good friend of Joseph Kennedy's that he celebrated JFK's presidential victory with the family in Hyannis Port, was named Morton Downey. When the son was interviewed for the first edition of *The Pink Palace,* he called himself Sean Morton Downey and identified himself as a member of the Democratic National Committee. By the end of the eighties, he had transformed himself into Morton Downey, Jr., a rightwing, TV rabblerouser who was to drape Old Glory over his rear end and instruct an Iranian guest to "kiss my flag."

Admittedly the movie and social stars staying in the bungalows for months on end were not big spenders. Their presence, however, brought in those who tipped well, ran up large restaurant and room service bills, and shopped in the arcade. Having Elizabeth Taylor and Baroness de Goldschmidt-Rothschild wafting through the gardens gave the hotel the imprimatur of glamour and style.

Not all the celebrities spotted at the Hills were staying there. Some lived nearby and dropped in to pick up their newspapers at the drugstore and read them in the coffee shop. (Before the introduction of satellite-feeds to far-flung printing plants, people would reserve a copy of Sunday's *New York Times,* which would come in a day or two late. There would be a great row if someone tried to make off with someone else's copy.) Many of the locals treated the hotel as their club, an attitude Courtright encouraged.

One of his more clever moves was turning the pool into a swimming club, with an annual community membership of two hundred. The way it was set up, the club and not the hotel owned the green and white cabanas. At one point, actor-turned-conservative politician George Murphy shared one with Robert Montgomery. Silent-film star Anita Stewart had another. Hotel guests were given temporary membership as long as they were registered.

The Sand and Pool Club was officially opened in April 1940 with a party sponsored by the Beverly Hills Flower Club. "Party" is something of a misnomer for this was no small cocktails-and-chrysanthemum affair. It was an extravaganza with an aquatic circus, a fashion show courtesy of Saks Fifth Avenue, and exhibition tennis matches.

There actually was sand at the Sand and Pool Club. Sunbathing fanatics, in this more gentle time before we worried about ultraviolet exposure and skin cancer, swore there was a qualitative, if not quantitative difference between a poolside and an oceanside tan (the latter being better). They maintained sand was the determining factor. So that no one could claim to have gotten an inferior tan at the Beverly Hills Hotel, bright white sand was imported from Arizona for a special sunning section. Many neighborhood children, since grown up, recall long hours playing in what they considered their sandbox. Even without the sand, the pool would have been a success. Its location at the west end of the property, positioned to the sun, makes it as close to ideal as possible.

Courtright had been told to save the hotel or sell it. By 1940 it was well on the way to recovery. At Christmas that year, profits had increased so much that Courtright was able to give the entire 118-member staff a bonus, equaling about a third of a month's salary. It had been, he said, "a very successful year."

The long Depression had finally ended for the hotel, in large part because of Courtright's efforts. He could have walked away at that point, his mission accomplished, and returned to banking, where he had a promising future; everyone said so.

But having worked so hard and enjoyed it so much, what he did was inevitable. He was later to complain that Beverly Hills residents "never believe in our own things. We always sell something to a fellow from Des Moines or Cincinnati, and he turns around and makes a fortune." Why should some Midwestern bankroller, with no feel for the hotel or the town, take over for no other reason than he had cash to spare? Why not sell it to someone who appreciated the value of the property beyond the bottom line.

In 1943 Courtright did precisely that. He sold it to himself...and a few of his friends. These were nice Beverly Hills friends, an aristocratic mixture of stars and tycoons.

Raiding the top drawer of Our Lady of the Cadillac, Courtright brought together Irene Dunne and her husband, Dr. Francis Griffin; Loretta Young and her husband, Tom Lewis, an advertising executive who handled Young and Rubicam's radio accounts; Will Hays, onetime postmaster general, better remembered as head of the movie censorship office set up by the Motion Pictures Producers and Distributors of America after the Fatty Arbuckle scandal; Tom Hamilton, an airline executive who had been with the United Aircraft Company and Hamilton Standard Propeller; Willard Keith, president of the largest insurance-brokerage house on the West Coast; the internationally famous tap-dancing team of Tony and Sally DeMarco; Verbena Hebbard, whose name appeared regularly in society columns; Joseph Schnitzer, treasurer of the Hollywood Turf Club; and Harry Warner, one of the four brothers.

Courtright described it as "one of those deals that comes once in a decade." What made it such a great deal was not only the property but the investors as well. They made it, in Courtright's words, "a good buy." The hotel became more than where the stars came for a drink. It was now Irene Dunne and Loretta Young's place. The new owners were influential in Beverly Hills, and they had lots of friends. It seemed natural for friends to stay at a friend's place.

It also seemed natural for Hernando Courtright to hand in his resignation to the Bank of America.

Wartime.

The residents of Beverly Hills felt they were on the country's first line of defense. The president as much as said so soon after Pearl Harbor.

In early 1942 he warned the country that "Enemy ships could swoop in and shell New York; enemy planes could drop bombs on war plants in Detroit; enemy troops could attack Alaska."

"But aren't the army and navy and air force strong enough to deal with anything like that?" he was asked.

"Certainly not," was his answer.

Beverly Hills was close to the coast and vulnerable. The Japanese had already proved their treachery on the day that would live in infamy, so why should those living near the Pacific coast feel secure? To reinforce the fear and paranoia, a rogue Japanese submarine shelled an oil refinery seven miles north of Santa Barbara, only ninety miles from Los Angeles. The submarine inflicted little damage on the refinery but was more successful in destroying the nerves of motorists on the Coast Highway. One shell skimmed the tops of cars on the jammed road before smashing into a hillside.

It was obvious that no one and no place was safe from this despicable enemy and that every good American would have to stand strong and make sacrifices to defeat the Japanese. With that in mind, John Barrymore called the Beverly Hills police chief late one night to volunteer his swimming pool for active duty. The Great Profile would drain his pool so that it could be used as an antiaircraft emplacement. His offer was turned down—probably no one wanted him that close to a loaded machine gun—but several other pools were emptied for just that purpose.

There was no escaping reminders that a war was on—soldiers in uniform were everywhere, even at the front desk of the Beverly Hills Hotel. Clerks were on leave, others were about to be shipped out. People became so accustomed to seeing uniforms, they stopped giving them a second thought—until they got a glimpse of one that paraded through the hotel lobby in 1943.

The incident began innocently enough at a Hollywood restaurant. As was his custom, Gene Fowler was having a bit to drink with lunch. Instead of having a soothing effect, the alcohol was like kerosene fueling the writer's fiery anger with his employers, the brothers Warner. They were no good Philistines who wouldn't appreciate good writing if Shakespeare submitted a script. They were...With each drink, Fowler's tirade grew louder. Finally, probably to shut him up, someone at the table informed him that at that very moment, the brothers and their executives were discussing his contract.

That was too much. Fowler would take no more. He got in his car and drove—as steadily as he could—to the studio in Burbank. With the devil and large volume of 80 proof in him, Fowler would show them. At the door to the conference room, he whipped off his pants and carried them in. "Look, Jack," he said with great hauteur, "I want these cleaned, pressed, and back by three."

The Warner brothers had been tailors in an earlier life and didn't like to be reminded of it, especially not by someone on their payroll. Fowler was fired on the spot.

In search of sympathy, Fowler drove to the home of his friend, cartoonist Gladys Parker. She could be relied on to give him a commiserative drink. Perhaps to take his mind off his woes, having already filled his glass, Parker pulled out of the closet a gift she had recently received from a war correspondent. It was a Nazi overcoat, replete with insignia and accompanying paraphernalia.

Fowler was delighted and asked to borrow the coat to show his wife, which was all he set out to do. On the way home, however, wearing the German uniform, he passed the Beverly Hills Hotel. Wasn't Harry Warner one of the owners? Wasn't he mad at Harry Warner and his cretin brothers? Fowler took a sharp turn into the hotel's driveway. Up he drove, out he leapt, into the lobby he goosestepped, yelling that the Nazis had taken over Beverly Hills.

It was such a convincing performance that many people fled in terror.

A drunk Gene Fowler creating panic was the least of the hotel's problems. One of its biggest was staying adequately staffed. Hotels, like so many other businesses, lost their employees to the Selective Service. Even though people were clamoring for rooms, and many hotels had 100 percent occupancy, entire floors had to be shut because there wasn't staff enough to service them. Some hotels were forced to close altogether. (The Stevens in Chicago, the largest hotel in the world, ran into problems of an entirely different sort—it ran into the military. The army had bought it and then proceeded to mismanage it into the ground. With great embarrassment, the hotel would be sold in 1943 at a tremendous loss.)

If staffing was a challenge, finding guests was not. The war suddenly gave jobs to people who were begging for work five years earlier. The war also made it hard for people to spend their newly earned money since industry and effort was going into beating the Axis and not consumer goods and services. People wanted to spend their excess cash, so they traveled, even though travel was an unpredictable undertaking during the war. Gas rationing made car trips difficult. Buses, trains, and planes were iffy since a citizen never knew when he or she would be bumped by someone holding a wartime priority.

(A minor scandal had erupted when three servicemen, two on emergency furloughs to see gravely ill wives, lost their places on a flight because of a number-one priority cargo. There was outrage when the priority cargo turned out to be Blaze, a pedigreed English bull mastiff, belonging to the president's son, Elliott Roosevelt and his wife, actress-socialite Faye Emerson.)

Many travelers got stuck in terminals and depots across the country, unable to reach their destinations. Even if they did, as Cabell Phillips wrote in his *1940s—Decade of Triumph and Trouble*,

"...there was always the gambler's luck in finding a hotel room, reservations to the contrary notwithstanding. Desk clerks were easily overwhelmed by the sudden appearance of a clutch of exuberant young officers in town on a three-day pass, or by peremptory demands from Washington to make way for an emergency session of the Nut and Bolt Manufacturers' War Council .... In some cities, and this was particularly true in resorts like Miami and Santa Barbara, the military commandeered entire hotels for long periods, using them as rest and transient facilities and even as residential quarters for men stationed at nearby posts."

Living quarters of all types were in short supply as workers crowded into industrial centers where they could find jobs but no housing. Even the Plaza in New York was a victim to overcrowding. Cots were installed in managers' offices for the overflow, although the cot-guests were told, with regret, that they would have to vacate by nine so that the managers could start work.

The Beverly Hills was spared being overrun by the military. On the contrary, when top brass were in town for conferences with aircraft executives, the executives registered at the Hills, while the generals were relegated to lesser establishments.

Not that military personnel never stayed at the hotel. In 1942 Private Pat de Cicco checked in while on furlough from Fort Bliss. He wasn't alone, however. Accompanying him was his bride, Gloria Vanderbilt de Cicco. Furthermore, de Cicco wasn't to be low man on the military totem pole for long—he was on his way to officer-training school in New Jersey.

If the Beverly Hills didn't help the war effort by serving as a barracks, it was the site of many lucrative war-bond drives. While not everyone could sacrifice a pool to defeat Hitler, many could contribute money. There would be Buy a Bomber breakfasts at which the purchase of a thousand-dollar bond got you ham, eggs, and Eddie Cantor. And war-bond aquacades. One starred Ann Curtis, a five-foot-ten-inch swimmer, whose seven national championships and nineteen national swimming records had earned her the country's top amateur sports honor, the Sullivan Award.

Opening festivities for the area's first USO were held at the hotel. For all the success of these events, nothing matched what happened in Gimbel's bargain basement. Danny Kaye was emcee at an auction of historical memorabilia—a letter written by George Washington, Thomas Jefferson's personal Bible, and the like. One of the "likes," of lesser historical significance, was the violin Jack Benny had played without mercy, for twenty years, in his act. Kaye received a written bid for it.

A one-million-dollar war bond.

Naturally, the bid caused an uproar with everyone wanting to know who this patriotic Benny fan was. Even after his name was announced, few had ever heard of him. Julius Kornfein was a Russian immigrant who had built a small Brooklyn cigar shop into the gigantic Garcia Grande Cigar Company. The million-dollar bond was a show of appreciation and support for his adopted country in its time of need.

With the war came ration books, skimping, and deprivation—even for the privileged who frequented the Beverly Hills. Rationing meant making do or finding some way to sidestep the regulations without making yourself feel guilty for undermining the war effort. Many people rationalized that the decrees were so complicated and capricious that some cheating was needed to make the rationing system work.

It was practically a fulltime occupation trying to keep up with the rationing rules, the new, superceding rationing rules, and the revised-until-May-then-we'll-revert-to-January rationing rules.

One Office of Price Administration guideline read as follows:

"Blue Stamps in War Ration Book No. 2 are used for most canned goods and for dried peas, beans, lentils, and frozen commodities like fruit juice. The Red Stamps are used for meats, canned fish, butter, cheese, edible fats, and canned milk. You have to give up more points when buying scarce food than when buying the same quantity of a more plentiful one ....

"Red Stamps J, K, and L may be redeemed through June 20. Blue Stamps G, H, and J are valid through June 7, and Blue Stamps K, L, and M are valid through July 7. Ration stamps are not valid if detached from their appropriate books.

"Each person has a Red Stamp quota of 16 points a week (meats, cheese, butter, etc.) allowing an average of approximately two pounds per week per person. Each person has 48 points in blue Stamps (most processed foods) to expend between June 6 and July 2 ....” and so on, through bureaucratic gobbledygook ad infinitum.

Of course, having your ration stamps didn't always mean you'd get what you wanted. An example was butter, which rarely reached store shelves. The dairy industry had jumped at an early opportunity to sell exclusively to the armed forces at an extremely high price. This left civilians, with or without the proper Red Stamp, staring at an empty spot in the dairy case.

Congress, trying to improve the situation, gave the margarine industry special dispensation to precolor its pasty-gray product to a buttery-looking yellow. Dairymen had successfully fought precoloring for years. When a consumer bought margarine, a package of yellow coloring was included. It was a lot easier to buy butter.

Since there was none during the war, margarine was touted as a satisfactory substitute. People got used to it and many didn't want to switch back after the war. State legislatures were pressured into allowing precoloring until only Wisconsin was left with gray margarine.

Beverly Hills matrons, a sly lot, came up with a clever circumvention of meat rationing. The hotel's room service would receive calls from the cooks of these matrons, who while strictly speaking were not guests of the hotel, did patronize it. The cooks would place an order—a popular request was for “pork chops, blue”—and later pick up the raw meat at the kitchen door.

This was not a good time for lovers of fine food, as the new magazine *Gourmet* pointed out. Nor was it a great time for such a magazine to begin publication. Its editors had planned to run articles on eating holidays in Provence and pack its pages with recipes for truffle sauces. Instead they had to urge readers to plant home spice gardens, help China by buying almond cookies from the United China Relief, substitute blue cheese for Roquefort, and eat more game—

"Although it isn't/our usual habit/This year we're eating/The Easter rabbit." And out of necessity, *Gourmet* extolled the delights of making do with California *vin ordinaire*.

There wasn't much else one could get. Drinkers of hard liquor were also hit with a long dry spell. The country was barely accustomed to the end of Prohibition and being able to buy alcohol in a store and not a dark alley when the war began and Scotch imports ended. As the existing supplies were depleted, Scotch drinkers were prepared to switch to American-distilled brews, such as bourbon, only to discover that alcohol was used to make gunpowder, and gunpowder had higher priority than sour mash.

The order came down in October 1942: American distillers were forbidden to make drinking alcohol until further notice—June 1944, it turned out. American ingenuity did manage to get an experimental blend out earlier in 1944—made from surplus and waste potatoes—but it was $3.32 a fifth, a small fortune, and there wasn't enough of it to go around. It wasn't until mid-1946 that Scotch began showing up in appreciable amounts on American liquor shelves.

Except at the Beverly Hills, which never ran out. As the rest of the country made do with beer (beer production was deemed vital to the war effort—making airplanes and bombs could work up a powerful thirst), regulars at the hotel were never without their spirit of choice. Legend has it Courtright had seen to that by taking a timely grand tour of European vineyards and distilleries, immediately prior to the outbreak of hostilities. Included on his itinerary were out-of-the-way monasteries where monks passed the centuries concocting wonderful liqueurs. He bought everything he could ship back, making a particularly thorough sweep of Reims, the center of the Champagne district. Back in Beverly Hills, these purchases were stored in every available closet and cellar and even behind secret panels.

Despite Courtright's efforts, the hotel's Scotch supply got dangerously low as the war dragged on. Finally, Courtright went to Will Hays and asked him to prevail upon his friend Joseph Kennedy, who had been ambassador to Great Britain, to see what he could do to keep glasses filled at the Polo Lounge. Before long cases of Old Parr—not much of a Scotch, but Scotch nonetheless—were being delivered to the hotel.

There was a picture taken in 1948 in the hotel's Rodeo Room. Outside the floor-to-ceiling windows towering palm trees are silhouetted in marigold sunshine. Inside four people relax in low easy chairs in front of a low easy table. At one side is a cooler with a wine bottle in it; at the other, a white-jacketed waiter bends to serve. In the center of the picture, in one of the easy chairs, Maurice Chevalier is smiling, lounging comfortably, caught in that fraction of perfect time.

1948 was a good year for the Beverly Hills Hotel. During one week the guest registry listed Beatrice Lillie; Lily Pons and Andre Kostelanetz; the Philippine ambassador to the United States, Joaquin M. Elizade; English Labour Party leader in the House of Lords, Lord Strabolgi; magazine publishing magnate Gardner Cowles; ex-regent of Siam, Prince Banoyoung; and a party of Arabian princes who insisted on stationing burnoosed guards outside their suites.

(A hotel barber was called on to shave the princes, an unenviable task seeing that the guards first checked his razor then carefully watched every stroke he took. "It made me kind of nervous, and the once-over lightly I gave him was *very* light!")

In the lobby you were likely as not to bump into Danny Kaye, Dorothy Lamour, Katharine Hepburn, Walter Huston, Sinclair Lewis, Edgar Bergen, Raymond Massey, Elizabeth Taylor, Evelyn Keyes, Paulette Goddard, Hedy Lamarr,

Aristotle Onassis, who spent two years at the hotel when the war prevented him from living in Greece.

Al Jolson shared Bungalow 4 with his then-wife Erle. Maxwell Anderson came to the hotel in search of Ingrid Bergman, who he wanted to star in his play *Joan of Lorraine.* Anderson was either an innocent or someone completely removed from the news of the day. He had decided Bergman must be his Maid of Lorraine, without realizing she was already a major film star. He got her phone number, delivered the script, and said he needed an immediate response. If for nothing else, she was impressed by his audacity, read the play, and accepted the role.

Who you weren't going to see at the hotel was Van Johnson, Hollywood's newest heartthrob. He was asked to leave the hotel when his boisterous fans tried to bribe elevator operators into telling them his room number.

The hotel did its best to keep boisterousness at a minimum. "We like to put our bachelor cottagers in [Bungalow] 14," the clerks would explain. "You know, pretty remote from the rest of the hotel in case of any little rumpus." (Over the years the number of bungalows had been increased from their original ten.)

The hotel was now an extension of Hernando Courtright, as it once had been of Margaret Anderson. His vision of the hotel became the hotel. It was he who instituted the unusually high staff-to-guest ratio—one and a half to one. He banned conventions. The Beverly Hills would have no "Hi! My Name's Harry"s running through the corridors. The closet thing to Shriners-time would be the subdued showing of new Rolls-Royces in the ballroom.

"A convention isn't considerate of those who aren't part of it," Courtright explained. "If you entertain a convention of fifty people, the whole hotel might just as well be in it." The ban was never relaxed. When the 1960 democratic nominating convention was in Los Angeles, the hotel did not hold any rooms for delegates. Only some of its "old friends," like Senator Stuart Symington, were accommodated. John F. Kennedy was officially registered at another hotel, however, he had a bungalow at the Hills for entertaining a steady stream of girlfriends, such as Judith Campbell Exner and Angie Dickinson.

Courtright also began a policy of an assistant manager "rooming" the guests—that is, he would escort them to their room and make sure it was to their liking instead of leaving that to a bellman.

Before guests got to their accommodations, a staff member would make certain all lights were on, windows open, and curtains drawn to allow a full appreciation of the view. At night it was the task of fifty maids to turn down the beds and lay out the guests' bed clothes.

Courtright went to great lengths for his guests' comfort. It was his idea to have private patios built off the first-floor rooms.

"We thought it would be nice if we could serve guests drinks in their own gardens, where they could even sunbathe in privacy."

There was one aspect to the plan that bothered him. Would noise from the patios disturb guests on the upper floors? To find out, he had an experimental patio put in outside his own room, threw a couple of parties, and waited for complaints. When none came, he okayed work on the other rooms.

Courtright's biggest contribution to the hotel's expansion was the Crescent Wing, a four-story addition that reshaped the hotel from a "T" to an "H." Although modern, with clean lines—and no ocher tiles on the roof—the addition blended nicely with the older section. Across its side was signatured BEVERLY HILLS HOTEL, so that anyone coming down Sunset Boulevard knew they were passing some place special.

(In 1951, the sign wasn't the only thing passersby noticed on the Crescent Wing. A millionaire real estate developer, Samuel Genis, and his wife, Sayde, were hanging laundry from the balcony railings of their four-room suite as well as putting the staff and other guests in a turmoil by "using obscene language, berating them, using loud and boisterous tones, dumping trash in the hallways." The hotel sued to have them evicted.)

Being the promoter that he was, Courtright coordinated the opening of the Crescent Wing with the California Centennial celebration in 1949.

In December, a parade of movie industry big names rode from City Hall to the hotel. Harold Lloyd. Pat O'Brien. Ann Miller. Maureen O'Sullivan. Claire Trevor. Leo Carrillo. George Murphy. Arlene Dahl. Victor Moore. John Mack Brown. Jean Hersholt. Alan Ladd. And leading the parade, Hopalong Cassidy and his faithful horse, Topper. While the state flag was hoisted by the mayor of Beverly Hills and the Sheriff's Boys Band played, with great fervor, "I Love California," Courtright released a balloon carrying a symbolic key to the new $1.5 million wing.

The town of Beverly Hills was also experiencing changes. In 1930 the population had been 17,400. By 1950, it was more than 29,000. What didn't change was that it was a town of older people. There were 18,472 people older than thirty-five. Of those, 10,544 were over fifty. Only 5,275 were under twenty.

And the town was still considered an appendage of Los Angeles, a conception Courtright wished to change.

Later he would recall, "The town has begun to move. It may be immodest to say so, but I think I gave it momentum. I had to get people over the idea that Beverly Hills was uptown Los Angeles. Almost every concept on which we predicated the Beverly Hills Hotel has been realized.

Beverly Hills is like Park Avenue or Fifth Avenue. We're sitting right in the middle of it—in the heart of Beverly Hills in the heart of Los Angeles."

This statement was made before Rodeo Drive had become the symbol of overconsumption and astronomical prices.

Courtright had made Beverly Hills his home and was deeply involved with the community. He founded the Beverly Hills Wine and Food Society and the California Chapter of the Chevaliers du Tastevin. He was a member of the Jurande de Saint Emilion, the Commanderie du Bontemps du Medoc, the West Hills Hunt Club, and the Beverly Hills Polo Club. In 1950 he was instrumental in forming the Los Angeles Hotel Association.

He was a man to whom both guests and staff had great loyalty and genuine fondness. There was a charming flamboyance to him, as he dressed in embroidered sombreros and serapes sometimes, and London-tailored shantung suits at others. Mrs. Samuel Goldwyn said of Courtright, "The days when movie stars and other Hollywood people used to turn up in elaborate costumes and getups are pretty much gone [she said this before Madonna and Cher], but Hernando carries on the great tradition. He's the last of Hollywood pashas."

Central Casting would have been proud.

chapter six

L ife would soon begin to imitate soap operas, for in entered Ben L. Silberstein, the one man who hated Hernando Courtright.

Silberstein had no exotic, romantic background. He was from Detroit, a lawyer turned businessman with nothing in his biography worth mentioning except in the financial pages. There were occasional whispers that he had been connected with the Michigan arm of the Mafia in his younger days; but Detroit lawyers were often rumored to have been connected with the Purple Gang.

Silberstein's son-in-law, Burton Slatkin, would dismiss the rumor as "completely absurd," pointing out that Silberstein "not only could hardly know, or have come in contact with, any member of the Purple Gang because they were born and raised in completely opposite sections of the city; in addition, Silberstein was a teenager and not a lawyer during the period of their notoriety."

Regardless, lawyering wasn't his main occupation. After getting his degree from the Detroit College of Law, he turned to real estate. When he was thirty, in 1933, Silberstein, with his brother Joseph, started putting together an impressive portfolio of property, mostly sites for chain stores. He didn't hesitate to diversify when something else came along. For instance, Silberstein bought the Universal Gear Works in 1942 and the Master Machinery and Gear Work in Oxford, Michigan, three years later.

In 1945, he closed a deal on the twenty-five-story National Bank Building in downtown Detroit, paying six million dollars for a property that had been listed at fifteen million. This brought to thirty-eight the number of business properties he and his associates controlled. Ostensibly a broker, he once told *Newsweek*, "We were always in every deal. We'd occasionally take a commission but only when we had to."

Everything was a deal to Silberstein. The word punctuated his conversations, not surprising if he was to do well in real estate. He had to keep his sensors finely tuned for prospects which might materialize unexpectedly and where he least expected them.

There is no reason to believe that Silberstein was expecting the great life change that came when he decided to visit Southern California in the early fifties. It was a trip to Los Angeles, nothing more. He thought he might stay at the Beverly Hills Hotel. When he tried to get a reservation, he was surprised to learn it was completely booked, although he was traveling in what was considered the off-season. Silberstein made a mental note to check out this busy—and presumably profitable—place when he had a chance. Who knew? It might be a good deal.

Silberstein was not a complete stranger to the hotel business, at least not to the buying-selling-speculating end of it. At one point, he had owned the Pantalind in Grand Rapids, Michigan, and had considered going after the Hotel Pierre in New York. (He passed on that after deciding the city's strict rent control laws would put a damper on profits.)

The Beverly Hills Hotel whetted his interest. On his next trip to the West Coast, accompanied by his wife and teenage daughters, Muriel and Seema, Silberstein managed to get rooms. He liked what he got. And he liked what he saw. As did Muriel. She was supposed to have turned to her father and said, "Daddy, you buy everything else. If you want me to be interested in your business, why don't you buy this hotel?"

As Muriel was to tell it some thirty years later, "The legend is absolutely true. I was seventeen years old, and I had never been in California. So my father planned a trip and booked two adjoining rooms .... When we arrived, the hotel was full; they put us in a bungalow, and I fell in love—with the place. And so, yes, the legend is true. I did actually say, 'Daddy, why don't you buy us this hotel.'"

Silberstein found it an interesting enough idea to at least approach the owners.

He sent out a feeler. Would the owners consider selling and for how much?

An answer came back.

They would consider no offer. The Beverly Hills was not for sale at any price. Period.

The response was so emphatic that Silberstein dropped the matter. Not everything could be bought.

A year passed. It was fall 1953, in Detroit. Silberstein was taking care of business when an associate approached him for a loan. More as a personal favor than anything else, Silberstein gave him the money.

The business associate was greatly appreciative. "If there's anything I can ever do for you, please let me know," he said.

A bell went off. Silberstein remembered that the associate had a friend who had a friend who happened to be none other than Dr. Francis Griffin, Irene Dunne's husband. Both were members of the syndicate that owned the Beverly Hills Hotel. The hotel that wasn't for sale. Period.

Sometimes periods, with the help of friends and friends of friends, can be transformed into ellipses or commas or question marks. Silberstein asked the associate if his friend might be able to encourage Dr. Griffin to talk with Silberstein.

Surprise, surprise. Not only would Dr. Griffin talk, he sent back a price.

Five and one-half million dollars. Today that will only get you one house in the hotel's neighborhood, and not the largest one, either. But in the early fifties, it was a very high, almost outrageous, amount to be asking.

The question was, why the asking price at all? What had happened between the first and second feelers? Had the hotel syndicate responded only out of courtesy to the associate's friend, lobbing back such a high figure to discourage Silberstein? Was there a fight among syndicate members, and they no longer wished to be associated with each other? Had the San Andreas Fault shifted to directly under the hotel?

Or was Conrad Hilton coming to town?

Hilton: a name to strike fearsome visions of receivership into competitors. Next to Cesar Ritz, his name more than any other meant hotel. His worldwide chain was so vast and widely known that it was half-expected the first astronauts on the moon would find a Lunar Hilton in place.

Word was out. Hilton was unloading the Plaza in New York, which he'd owned since 1943. This so that he might build a twelve-million-dollar luxury hotel in Beverly Hills. Though many of Hilton's hotels had a monotonous uniformity that made people wonder if they were in the Far East or the Midwest, he did have a flair for publicity (he married Zsa Zsa Gabor, after all) and attracting guests. Hilton was the type of operator who tried to cover all the angles. At the Plaza, he hired Prince Serge Obolensky to again attract the younger society set which had once made the hotel their hangout. The prince was one of them and would have been a regular in the columns even if he hadn't married John Jacob Astor's daughter. Hilton was proved right; and the Plaza was again *the* place to go.

Would Hilton use similar techniques to lure away the Beverly Hills' faithful?

The specter of the new hotel didn't overwhelm the Beverly Hills' syndicate, but it did make them pause, at least long enough to listen to this man from Detroit who seemed so terribly interested in their lovely little investment. Tell him five and a half million and see what he does.

With this modicum of encouragement, Silberstein got serious. He flew to Beverly Hills to take a closer look, as any prudent businessman would. He inspected the buildings. He observed operations. He examined the books. He walked the grounds and figured there was "about a million bucks' worth of landscaping....It took half a century for those palm trees to grow. You just can't put them in that way...."

Silberstein went to other hotels in the area to see how they were doing and how they did things. When his tour was finished, he was sure the competition, present and future, wouldn't bother him. If for no other reason, the Beverly Hills Hotel's location in a beautiful residential area gave it an advantage. The only other four-star hotel in such an area was the Gerhus, set in a wooded section of Berlin.

To Silberstein, the Beverly Hills Hotel was invulnerable. "Here's this beautiful hotel planted right in the center of this residential area like a little gem. Nobody can build a hotel in Beverly Hills in a district like this one. They can build on Wilshire Boulevard, where it is surrounded by a lot of commercial atmosphere, a lot of traffic, and a lot of other factors that make it clearly a commercial hotel. But the Beverly Hills...blends into an area that is completely luxurious and uncommercial by itself. You've got the beauty and quiet of home living right here, but in a hotel."

No matter how he added, subtracted, multiplied, or divided, Silberstein kept coming up with a million dollars a year gross—easy.

And yet, five and a half million was clearly far too much for the property. The price had to be an opening gambit. The owners would take less. It was time to negotiate.

Representatives for the two sides, seven in all, sequestered themselves and haggled for three days, but at the end of the exhausting session, the price was still five and a half million.

To break the impasse, Silberstein himself sat down at the bargaining table, confident he could make the deal.

The price didn't budge.

In retrospect, Silberstein figured those dollar signs in his eyes must have been shining too brightly. The hotel's representatives knew he would give in.

He did.

Those in the know thought it was a stupid deal. Then again, those in the know thought it was stupid deal for Burton Green and Mrs. Anderson.

"When we bought it for five and a half million," Silberstein said, "everyone said I was nuts. William Zeckendorf and the twenty other guys who buy properties all figured it was a mad deal. Those wise guys said I went overboard." (Of course, the wise guys couldn't have imagined the California land boom of the seventies and eighties, which sent property values into the stratosphere. Five and a half million for the hotel would later look like winning the lottery.)

Silberstein was willing to overpay. He was bullish on Southern California, and he wanted the hotel. Let Conrad Hilton come; he could spend millions, and when he was done, he would have a hotel. Ben L. Silberstein would have a legend.

This appeared in the *Los Angeles Times* on January 23, 1954:

"Hernando Courtright, president and general manager of the Beverly Hills Hotel Corp. announced yesterday that Ben L. Silberstein, Detroit investor and real estate owner, has acquired a substantial stock position in the hotel company. . . .

Courtright will continue to operate the Beverly Hills Hotel as president and general manager and 'all policies that have brought the hotel international recognition will be continued.'"

So there it was, in black and white and the *LA Times*. Ben L. Silberstein and his two daughters now owned 80 percent of the privately owned and closely held Beverly Hills Corporation. Silberstein had raised the money for the deal from prominent Detroiters—Mrs. Eugene Arnfeld, Norman Hayden, Sidney Weissman, Mrs. Anna Srere, Donald Krotkin, Louis Blumberg, Mrs. Irving Blumberg. Names that meant something in Detroit, but lacked the magic of Irene Dunne, Loretta Young, or even Verbena Hebbard.

The syndicate had done exactly what Courtright complained about. It had sold to the "fellow from Des Moines or Cincinnati" who then "turns around and makes a fortune."

Not that Courtright's syndicate had done so badly. According to him, they received a hundred to one return on their investment.

With the sale completed, Silberstein and Courtright turned their attention to Conrad Hilton. At the end of June 1954, the Beverly Hills Corporation filed a suit in California Superior Court charging that the name *Beverly Hilton* would create unfair competition. The name, they contended, would cause "confusion and conflict" in the minds of people who might check into the Beverly Hilton thinking it was the Beverly Hills. The name Beverly Hilton, they said, would "mislead and deceive the public" and be an infringement on the rights of the Beverly Hills Hotel Corporation.

The Hilton lawyers filed their response in August, submitting eighteen affidavits, some as long as one hundred pages. Their contention was simple: *Beverly* was a geographical name, as in Beverly Hills. Conrad Hilton always named his hotels in the same manner—the location followed by his name: the Havana Hilton, the New York Hilton, the Wherever Hilton. Hence, the Beverly Hilton, the Beverly Hills Hilton was simply too much of a tongue twister. Further, Hilton lawyers showed 147 telephone directory listings with the word "Beverly" in them. Of those, five were hotels.

Superior Court Judge Allen T. Lynch ruled in Hilton's favor—a geographical name could not be copyrighted.

The Beverly Hilton, name intact, opened in August 1954. It was built on the busy corner where Wilshire and Santa Monica Boulevards meet, where there had once been a nursery and a "sock'em" golf range.

As it turned out, the Beverly Hilton had little effect on the Beverly Hills. The banquet business at the Hills fell off in the first nine months after the Hilton opened, but picked up after that.

If Hernando Courtright had been expecting the new cigar-smoking owner to be a long-distance, absentee landlord, he was in for a disappointment. From the start, Silberstein was hands-on and very much in attendance.

"For ninety days after I purchased the hotel, I made a personal survey of every department and came up with a program of improvement. I decided that the hotel, to maintain its great charm, had to remain small. We had to improve on what we had—make it the best. There are enough people who want the best and will pay for it.

"The hotel was basically in poor physical condition. The main building was forty years old, the plumbing and wiring were in bad shape, and the furnishings were second rate." The plumbing was in such bad shape that guests couldn't rely on having hot water for their showers and baths. (Ernest Brown, the hotel's assistant manager for many years, had a theory on why people put up with such inadequate facilities. "The homes of most of these people were nicer than the hotel. For them it like going on a camping trip.")

Silberstein was willing to spend money on improvements. For the next ten years he would put all profits back into the hotel. By 1964, five million dollars had been spent on physical improvements and about one million on new furnishings.

The ancient plumbing was replaced with modern sinks, tubs, and showers. Rooms were redecorated, each differently. New wiring was installed, as was a new heating system. Forty-five thousand dollars was spent to convert a downstairs conference room into a screening room. The kitchen was modernized, and window-mounted air conditioners were installed in many rooms.

(The Crescent Wing, with its big picture windows, was not air conditioned. Suite 486, the favorite of RCA's General David Sarnoff, was in that section of the hotel. Unfortunately, General Sarnoff was very partial to air conditioning. Whenever he came, a 220-volt line was run to 486 for an air conditioning unit that stayed in for as long as he did. At the same time, the television set that was usually in the room was switched for an RCA model, purchased especially for his visits.)

Silberstein also remembered "intensifying the services, replacing the people who weren't doing a first-rate job. Our employees must be cordial but not intimate—they must anticipate the services of a guest."

In some quarters there had been fears that the pragmatic businessman might go for quicker profit by cutting back on Courtright's service-intensive, cater-to-the-guest approach. If anything, Silberstein expanded on it.

The hotel became world-famous for pampering its guests—and you didn't have to be the founder of RCA to get "the Beverly Hills Treatment."

At its peak in the seventies and early eighties, some five hundred people worked at the hotel, serving no more than 275 guests in 325 rooms. There were 21 switchboard operators, 30 kitchen workers, 16 bellmen, 10 full-time gardeners, along with desk clerks, managers, maids, maitre d's, waiters, and others.

To track guests' preferences, the hotel kept a vast, color-coded card system. On the cards were noted what the guests liked to drink, their favorite rooms, how hard they like their mattresses, previous special requests, any complaints—sometimes into a mind-boggling level of minutiae.

The cards with the least amount of information on them and with the lowest ranking in the hotel pecking order were white. White cards were for first-timers who hadn't made the cover of *Time*, people with whom the hotel was unfamiliar. There was usually little on these cards beyond name, address, and credit information. When the hotel was overbooked—which was often—white cards were "farmed" first (an industry term for finding a room for them in another hotel). Lowest among the white cards were newlyweds, the rationale being that it probably would be quite some time before they could afford to return. Samuel Bronfman II, heir to the Seagram's fortune, was farmed on his wedding night. Even the notoriety of having been kidnapped a year earlier didn't save his room.

Most hotel guests were blue cards. Naturally, the greater the number of visits, the more notations were made.

Silberstein once called the cards a gimmick, albeit a nice one. People like being remembered and greeted with a "Mr. Jones, so nice to see you again. It's been seven months now, hasn't it? We've put you in Room 375 again since you enjoyed it so much on your last visit."

You were not anonymous at the Beverly Hills. The fact that you registered would reach the telephone operators before you could reach your room. Pick up the phone and the operator would say, "Yes, Mr. Smith. What number would you like?"

The Very Very Important People rated pink cards, but the hotel's perception of VIPs did not always coincide with that of the rest of the world. Being famous, rich, and powerful didn't automatically grant you pink-card status. Lyndon Baines Johnson started out on a white card and was elevated to blue primarily, it was said, because of Lady Bird's family and money and not his position in Washington. Indeed, when he became vice-president, his new occupation was noted in the space for "occupation," but he stayed a blue card. After John F. Kennedy's assassination, the "vice" was crossed off.

Some card notations were little more than common sense, such has putting an RCA set in Sarnoff's room, or making sure King Gillette didn't find any Schick razor blades in his bathroom.

Commander Whitehead always found bottles of Schweppes, with which he was associated, as well as a bottle of Beefeater gin in the bar in his room. And since he liked early morning swims before the pool opened, he was given a key to the gate.

Van Johnson, who was allowed back in the hotel in his post-heartthrob era, only got red napkins. Robert Mitchum was automatically served his morning wake-me-up of bourbon, orange juice, eggs, and honey (although that would have put most people to sleep).

Elizabeth Taylor always found pistachios in her room, and when she was married to Richard Burton, a fresh bucket of ice was delivered every hour. The cook saved the heels of French bread for actor Laurence Harvey.

In 1965 when Princess Margaret and then-husband Lord Snowdon came, the city was scoured for Gauloises, a French cigarette Snowdon smoked. When none could be found, the hotel had cartons flown in. The princess was served gin and tonic and he Scotch. Management found out what they liked for breakfast, and from morning one, the princess had her fresh fruit and rolls and he, eggs and ham. Both had tea made with distilled water.

It wasn't differences in hotelkeeping philosophy that led to the bitter animosity between Hernando Courtright and Ben Silberstein—for the hatred was mutual. The reason was far more basic: her name was Rosalind.

Silberstein had gone to the Beverly Hills on that initial trip with his two daughters and his wife. After the purchase, the wife didn't accompany Ben to California. The ensuing divorce was bitter and drawn-out, the kind that allows lawyers to retire early. As part of the settlement, Silberstein put the hotel in his daughters' names as well as his own.

(Even after Silberstein had packed up and moved out, he continued to send his dirty shirts back to Detroit. He liked the way his wife's maid did the laundry. When his ex-wife finally refused to accept any more, Ben made sure the Beverly Hills valet service rose to the standards of his former Michigan-maid. He would tell someone several years later, "My shirts cost twenty-eight dollars, and I want them to come back beautiful.")

Hernando Courtright also had a wife. She was a night-club singer whose career kept her on the road. It was sometime after Silberstein had bought the hotel and moved in before he met Courtright's wife—Rosalind.

They met on a mundane mission—some papers had to be signed. Who knows why or how these things happen. They just do. Soon Rosalind was spending more time with Ben than with Hernando—their marriage had been in trouble for a while.

It's almost inconceivable that one woman would have been attracted to two such different men.

Courtright was a bon vivant, charming, outgoing, a horseman, a gourmet, who not so much hobnobbed with society as society hobnobbed with him. Silberstein was closer to the chest; a high-stakes cardplayer who was often gruff; someone who laid down orders to the hotel staff that he was never to be addressed by his full name. Never, Mr. Silberstein, always, Mr. S. He didn't want guests to know who he was and that he owned the hotel. A guest asking the switchboard operator for Mr. Silberstein wouldn't be put through.

Courtright was a host, a man who enjoyed his guests and believed the customer was always right. Silberstein was more the master, a king who fiercely guarded his domain from people who didn't fit his idea of what a Beverly Hills guest should be and from those he plain didn't like.

A story was told of the time two young record producers, staying at the hotel, were talking with some disheveled and denimed friends in the lobby (one of whom was barefoot). They did not meet the Hills' dress code. When Silberstein spotted them, he loudly ordered a bellman to throw the rabble out.

The record producers protested. They were, after all, registered at the hotel, and who was this overbearing man to order their friends out?

The man explained that he was the owner of the Beverly Hills Hotel and that they were, from that moment, personae non gratae.

We're not leaving, said the producers, but we are calling our lawyer, and mentioned a famous, high-powered name.

Round one went to the record producers. They were allowed to stay, but something happened to their service. They no longer got the "Beverly Hills Treatment." In fact, life became downright unpleasant for them. The producers endured a few days, to make a point, then checked out.

Silberstein had a short temper which was triggered easily, sometimes for no discernible reason. A movie producer, a gentleman who had been at the hotel many times, was swimming in the pool. Silberstein happened to walk by —he walked religiously after many of his friends died from heart attacks. Suddenly he erupted. The producer had done something, he never could figure out what, that Silberstein didn't like, and Silberstein wanted him out of the pool and out of the hotel. Under the circumstances, the producer saw no reason to stay, but he always wondered what he had done.

It was estimated that the list of people unwelcome at the hotel eventually reached five hundred. Halston almost found himself on that list when he was at the height of his popularity, designing clothes for Jackie Kennedy, Liza Minnelli, and Bianca Jagger. He was in Los Angeles to escort Marisa Berenson, an aristocratic actress-model who appeared in *Cabaret* (her photographer sister, Barry, married Tony Perkins), to the Academy Awards ceremonies. Halston and his traveling companion, an Argentinian named Victor Hugo, had reservations at the Beverly Hills. On checking in, the desk clerk asked Halston for his full name—first *and* last.

"What are you talking about?" the designer sputtered. "I am Halston."

"Of course, sir," the clerk replied, "but I must have your entire name."

"It's Halston. Halston. My picture has been in *Time* magazine."

The clerk wouldn't budge—lots of people who registered at the hotel had their pictures in *Time,* but they signed in properly. Hugo finally took the pen and wrote in his companion's full name, R. Halston Frowick. If he hadn't, they wouldn't have been given the room, then or ever.

(Silberstein was not happy with this book when it was first published in 1978. One of the authors, Sandra Lee Stuart, was barred from the hotel. John Prince, who had been an employee of the Beverly Hills as well as a guest, kept his name off the title page to protect his friends still working at the hotel.)

Courtright and Silberstein's contrasting styles were evident with the staff, as well. Courtright was a man of effusive gestures. He would present his wine steward with an expensive silver sommelier cup as a gift.

Silberstein was Mr. S. One night auditor worked at the hotel for four years without receiving a single hello from him. There were many staff members who didn't like him—they found him abrasive and impatient. Silberstein would show up at the front desk four times a day, demanding his mail, tapping his fingers on the counter until he got it. He would sort through the envelopes and drop the ones he didn't care about on the floor for the desk clerk to pick up. One night, returning from dinner, he stopped at the bellman's desk to buy a paper. There was a new man on who, not speaking English well, made a mistake and got the papers mixed up. He asked Silberstein for a quarter. Silberstein started screaming, "You're fired. This paper only costs a dime."

Bud Bundy, the chief bellman, tried to intercede. It had to be a mistake; no one would risk their job for *fifteen* cents, after all. There was no reasoning with Silberstein; the bellman was out.

Not everyone at the hotel shared the low opinion of their boss. Nino Osti, host of the Polo Lounge for almost twenty-five years, was one who did not.

"Silberstein was a wonderful man if you did your job."

Nino could remember only one bad experience with Silberstein. It was hotel policy that before a guest was presented with a check, it was examined by the captain and then the cashier. One night a waiter did not follow procedure and gave Silberstein his check directly.

"Mr. S. looked it over and found it's two dollars short. He had an incredible head for figures."

He went over to Nino and berated him for the slip-up, in his loud voice, in front of the guests and other workers. Nino took the tongue-lashing in silence, but that night he could not sleep. He wrote Silberstein a letter, which he put in the hands of Mr. S.'s secretary, Eleanor, the next morning, admonishing her to give it only to Silberstein. That done, Nino waited for a response. None came that day. Nino didn't see Silberstein the next day, either. The third day, Nino found Silberstein's name on the reservation list. Okay, this would be it.

When Silberstein showed up, he asked Nino to sit with him in the lobby for a minute.

"Don't you ever write a letter like that to me again," Silberstein started.

Firmly, Nino restated his position. He was Mr. S.'s representative to the staff and the public. If Mr. S. had a complaint, he should call Nino into his office and tell him. He should never raise his voice like that again in public.

"Nino, you know I like you."

That wasn't the point. "Mr. S., I admit it when I make a mistake. There's no need to yell."

Silberstein grumbled an okay and went in to eat.

"Mr. S. was a gruff man but had a heart of gold. He never raised his voice to me again."

While there may not have been legions who would have agreed with the "heart of gold," it was Silberstein who instituted the semiannual bonuses, on July 1 and December 25, not Courtright.

Just to look at Courtright and Silberstein was to see men at opposite poles. Courtright dressed with flair, to be noticed. Silberstein favored old pants and knit shirts, dressing for himself and not for show. He would sit at his table in the Polo Lounge, fourth from the left against the wall, unnoticed, quiet, watching. Courtright wanted to be noticed, to greet, to have his name emblazoned across ads, menus, and matchbooks.

It's not that Silberstein was incapable of being gracious and generous. When he took a liking to British actor Michael York and his wife, two likable people, he ordered they "be given everything they want."

He could be generous in his donations. He presented the Detroit Museum of Art with a $150,000 Maillol sculpture and contributed $250,000 in his children's names to establish a pain clinic at Wayne State University. He gave the same amount to the UCLA Medical School.

And he always opened his wallet to his daughters. In 1965, unable to get permission from the Beverly Hills City Council to put up another 220 rooms on a triangular piece of property he acquired behind the hotel—where Katharine Hepburn parked her dog—he had built a showcase house for Muriel instead, a Regency-style mansion with a copper mansard roof. He set up Seema in an impressive Park Avenue apartment and filled it with fine furnishings and expensive artwork, when her husband could not afford to do so.

They were very different men, all right, Courtright and Silberstein. In temperament. In style. And throughout their lives they were always being measured against one another. One of Silberstein's admirers, his son-in-law Burton Slatkin, who was an executive at the hotel, seemed to resent comparisons between his father-in-law and Courtright. The difference between the two, he said, was that Silberstein was a direct, firm man. If he didn't like something, he would let you know, immediately and without subterfuge.

But Courtright, "he's sweet to your face" and then hits you with a memo written with a pen dipped in acid.

Perhaps Rosalind had tired of her husband's dissemblance. Sometimes knowing exactly where you stand with someone is refreshing and necessary. In any case, her relationship with Silberstein became common knowledge; it's hard to keep secrets in a hotel. The relationship between husband Courtright and lover Silberstein deteriorated until all communications ceased. Then the pettiness began. Silberstein would order a potted palm moved to this corner of the lobby. Courtright would spot it the next morning and order it moved to *that* corner. It was a bad time at the hotel and a relief for the staff when Courtright and Rosalind filed for divorce.

When the divorce was final, Rosalind married Silberstein.

No one who followed this version of *As The World Turns* was surprised when the *Los Angeles Times* reported on August 27, 1958:

"Hernando Courtright, colorful hotel figure, who has personally controlled and managed the Beverly Hills Hotel for 22 years, announced yesterday that he has resigned as president and director of the hostelry with the completion of a transaction in which the hotel was acquired by Benjamin Silberstein and associates, of Detroit. . . .

Courtright said he had made no decisions or commitments as to his future activities."

The sign of an institution. (*Gernot Kuehn*)

The Beverly Hills soon after it opened. That rutty road in the foreground is now the heavily trafficked Sunset Boulevard. (*Los Angeles Public Library*)

The hotel looking less forlorn a few years later. To the left is the old Toonerville trolley that carried guests and servants from the train station to the hotel. (*Los Angeles Public Library*)

Liza Minnelli at the front desk, 1970. She and her two cats took refuge at the hotel while her house was being painted. (*Ron Galella*)

It was a happy Halston in March, 1976, but he wasn't smiling the first time he came to the hotel. The designer was almost thrown out when he wouldn't sign his full name on the registry. (*Ron Galella*)

A table in the Polo Lounge was reserved exclusively for Charlie Chaplin, seen in here with *Modern Times* co-star and onetime wife, Paulette Goddard.

W.C. Fields (here with George Burns in *Six of a Kind* [1934]) once asked for and got a table for two in the Polo Lounge—for him and his man-eating plant.

Elizabeth Taylor's real-life father, Francis, had an art gallery downstairs in the Beverly Hills Hotel. Her reel father, Spencer Tracy, sometimes popped in for a drink in the thirties after a polo match.

Jean Peters gave up her short movie career to marry Howard Hughes and take up residence in one of several bungalows her eccentric husband rented. One of Peters' (left) few movies was *Three Coins in the Fountain* (1954) with Dorothy McGuire (right) and Maggie McNamara.

The Misfits (1961) was the last film for both Clark Gable and Marilyn Monroe. It was in the Polo Lounge that Arthur Miller talked Gable into taking the role.

Marilyn Monroe and Yves Montand did some off set rehearsing for *Let's Make Love* (1960) in Bungalow 5.

A scene from *Designing Women* (1957) with Lauren Bacall and Gregory Peck was shot at the Sand and Surf Club, one of the few times movie cameras were allowed to roll at the hotel.

Swooping off Sunset Boulevard up to the Beverly Hills. (*Gernot Kuehn*)

Silberstein made final payment on the hotel six months ahead of schedule. It was now his. A Detroit newspaper account reported Courtright had agreed to retire on receipt of the final payment. None of the stories mentioned Rosalind.

Courtright's departure and his own remarriage to a young Mexican woman, Marcelle Cuillery, brought no ceasefire. The animosity between Courtright and Silberstein never cooled. Courtright would act as if he couldn't remember "Silverberg's" name; Silberstein was an amnesiac when it came to Courtright. When the original edition of *The Pink Palace* was being researched in 1977, Courtright was approached about an interview. He wrote back, "I am not one bit interested in publicizing the Beverly Hills Hotel."

People say that Silberstein was no hotelman, that anyone with a modicum of business sense could have made a go of the Beverly Hills after Courtright had established it. The hotel was, nevertheless, Silberstein's, his palace, and Courtright had been deposed. Silberstein had taken queen and castle, and he had won the game. Checkmate.

Now it may be that Silberstein wasn't a hotelman, still he had enough sense and enough feeling for what he owned not to tamper with it. He could have gone for the fast buck, skimped a little here, gouged a little there, but he chose, instead, to maintain the standards of the hotel and use his money to raise them still higher.

Silberstein knew that the hotel catered to what he called the "top 2 percent." He believed in giving the guests the best, making them pay for it, but never shortchanging them. He insisted that only highest quality food be purchased and that his chefs were excellent. (Lyndon Baines Johnson offered one, Garry Reich, the prestigious job of White House chef. Reich turned it down.)

If Silberstein had let standards at the Beverly Hills slip, chances are Hernando Courtright would have won their rematch. He didn't go limping off to lick his wounded pride, never to be seen again. On the contrary, when given the chance to take on Silberstein, he seized it.

After leaving the Beverly Hills, Courtright hooked up with William Zeckendorf for a little project known as Century City. They envisioned a "Rockefeller Center West" of office buildings, stores, theaters, and restaurants, jutting up like the Emerald City, on a plot of land that had been the back lot of 20th Century-Fox.

It was a splendid idea, and one that would eventually be realized, but Zeckendorf and Courtright didn't have adequate funds to see it through. Century City, with its Avenue of the Stars, Century Plaza Hotel, and shopping mall, was finished by Alcoa.

Courtright, being Courtright, was not left on a short road to nowhere by the loss of the Century City project. It only meant he had to find something new.

As mentioned earlier, William Zeckendorf was one of the fifteen or twenty "guys who buy properties," guys who are usually into more than one deal at a time. Buy a parking lot here. Unload an apartment house there.

In 1955, in one of these fast shuffles, Webb and Knapp, the corporation Zeckendorf was with, ended up with the Gotham Hotel in New York and the Beverly Wilshire in California. (It also bought the lease to the Nacional in Cuba, a hotel owned by the Cuban government. Luckily for Webb and Knapp, they sold the lease to the Corporacion Intercontinental de Hoteles de Cuba, reportedly a subsidiary of Pan American World Airways, before Fidel Castro marched into Havana, making the lease worth less than the paper it was printed on.)

The Beverly Wilshire, while never falling into bankruptcy, had fallen on hard times. As writer Stephen

Birmingham put it, "It had become a hotel for convention-eers and itinerant drummers." Seedy, dilapidated, dreary. Webb and Knapp was more than happy to sell it to Courtright, who again got a little help from his friends, although this time he was to be the principal stockholder.

Again they were nice friends, friends like realtor Roger Stevens; Jimmy Stewart; Irene Dunne; former head of Magnavox, Richard O'Connor; Gregory Peck; Kirk Douglas; Earle Jorgensen, a big man in the steel industry; Henry Salvatori, a big man in the oil industry; Nils Onstad, a big man in Swedish industry and also Sonja Henie's husband; Edward Carter of the Broadway-Hale chain; Harry Volk of Union Bank; and the Walt Disney estate.

His dislike for Silberstein must have inspired him. Courtright set out to transform the Beverly Wilshire into a showcase that would outsplendor everything in Southern California.

The renaissance took place on a grand and costly scale. Not only would he redo the pseudo-Florentine palazzo (the first order of business was removing a garish neon sign from the roof), but he would build a 250-room, 10-story tower behind it, with a new "street" between the wings to make arrival by car easier. (Unloading and loading at the old entrance on busy Wilshire Boulevard had become a har-rowing operation.) The new tower, with interior decorations, ran seven million dollars over budget with a final cost of twenty-two million.

The overrun was due in part to Courtright's new wife, Marcelle, a perfectionist, who took over the hotel's deco-rating. She imported stonecutters from Italy to shape granite blocks for the hotel driveway. She bought wall hangings from one tribe of Mexican Indians and handmade boxes from another. (The only way to reach the second tribe was by helicopter.) She chose expensive French fabric for wall covering. Drapes in one room copied the pattern from a hanging in the Metropolitan Museum of Art in New York, to which royalties had to be paid.

One friend explained, "If there was one thing Hernando loved more than his hotel, it was Marcelle. He gave her complete freedom in terms of decor, and she went at it as though the sky was the limit."

The efforts paid off in a beautiful hotel that prided itself on the Courtright brand of service.

Marcelle, though many years younger than her husband, did not live to see the hotel completed. During her illness, Courtright gave up his favored wine for cranberry juice, for his health, he told people. He later confessed , "I wasn't telling the truth about the cranberry juice. There's nothing the matter with my kidneys, and you know how much I love my wine. But the other day I decided to give up wine—for Marcelle. I said to God, I'll give up everything I love the most, if you'll just let me keep Marcelle."

Courtright was to marry again. This wife, Florence Falzone, earned a dubious place in Beverly Hills social history. She sent out many invitations to a big party she was planning for French designer, Hubert Givenchy, neglecting to tell Givenchy about it.

"I don't know these people," the designer fumed. He refused to go, forcing cancellation of the party.

Things were not going well for Ben Silberstein back at the Beverly Hills. One big problem was his sister, Mrs. Hattie S. Sloan, to whom he hadn't spoken in years. In 1959, as reported by the *Detroit Free Press*, she renewed contact by suing him for allegedly mishandling their mother's trust fund.

Their mother, Mary, died in March 1941. Her estate was then worth $614,530 in personal property and real estate. Silberstein was named one of the trustees. According to sister Hattie, Ben was granted a loan for $71,274, using the mortgage on one of the trust properties as security. Some of the loan money *was* actually used to make improvements on the trust property. But, his sister charged, the rest was improperly used to acquire twenty-five thousand shares in the First National Bank Building. By law, any profits derived from a trust fund are supposed to go back to the fund. They didn't in this case, Hattie said. Furthermore, she charged that at about the same time Ben was negotiating purchase of the Beverly Hills Hotel, he had moved all the trust's cash into the account of the Silberstein Realty Company. He repaid this "loan" without interest.

"The co-mingling of funds of the Silberstein Realty Company with the trust fund is not conducive to proper management of the trust estate and is not in the best interest of the beneficiaries," Hattie's suit claimed.

In February 1965, the *Free Press* reported that the court had sided with sister Hattie.

Silberstein, said the story, "accused of mismanaging a million-dollar trust fund was ordered Friday to repay $737,000 to the trust.

"Circuit Judge Joseph A. Sullivan ordered Ben Silberstein, now of Palm Beach, Fla., to make the repayment to the estate of Silberstein's mother, Mrs. Mary Silberstein."

A year later the State of Michigan Appeals Court reduced the award to $109,990.95. Of course, Hattie did not receive the full sum. She had only a fifth interest in the trust, as did Ben. Further, according to Slatkin, "all of Hattie's charges of trust mismanagement, co-mingling of funds...were dismissed. The amount awarded was a compromise and was essentially a vindication of Ben's actions and position."

What must have pleased Courtright far more than Silberstein's sibling warfare was his marital one. The *Free Press* article had identified Silberstein as being "now of

Palm Beach" and that he was. The marriage to Rosalind had been a disaster, over as it began. Some cynics suggested the spark had gone out of the romance the moment Courtright exited. Be that as it may, the marriage was on the rocks. Unfortunately for Silberstein it was on the rocks in California, land of the fifty-fifty community-property settlement. He fled to Florida so that he wouldn't have to split his earnings for the period of the marriage. "Oh there was so much hatred," an observer noted. "She ran him out of the state."

One might think that having recently suffered bitter endings to two marriages, Ben Silberstein might have grown wary of Cupid's arrows. That wasn't the case. While living in Palm Beach, he met a beautiful former Broadway dancer named Bonita Edwards. Bonnie was not unfamiliar with the words in the wedding ceremony, having already married several times. One previous husband was many-times-a-groom Tommy Manville, whose family made its fortune manufacturing asbestos. It was the divorce settlement from Charles Wilson, a wealthy Englishman, that allowed her to become part of the posh Palm Beach society, a society established by Marjorie Merriweather Post when she realized the Blue Book would be closed to her in Boston, New York, and Philadelphia.

Once Rosalind was an "ex," Silberstein married Bonnie. Some fifteen or twenty years younger than Silberstein, Bonnie was one of those ageless women, unflappably cool and composed. She was a woman for whom no one—except maybe her stepdaughter Muriel—had an unkind word. The longtime night manager Ernie Brown, who kept in touch with Bonnie even after he left the hotel, recalled that "She never said anything negative about anyone even when things didn't please her. She could complain, but in a nice way. You got the feeling she was doing you a favor by complaining, that she was saying something only to help you out."

It was her equanimity that made it possible for her to stay married to the volatile Silberstein. Most other women would have left after he harangued her one day in the lobby and then slapped her hard enough to draw blood. Bonnie's reaction was to wordlessly take out a handkerchief and dab away the blood.

It is known that Bonnie reached her limit on at least one occasion. She had packed her bags and was on the way out when Slatkin intercepted her. Whatever he said made her turn around and return to her room. She didn't stay with Silberstein in hopes of a big inheritance. Some of the long-time switchboard operators, who were privy to many of the hotel's secrets, said Bonnie had signed a prenuptial agreement relinquishing all claims on Silberstein's estate.

If Silberstein had been looking for nothing more than a woman to project a good image for the hotel, he couldn't have done better than Bonnie. She was Town and Country, beige and cordial, easily able to make a gracious impression.

That their marriage never ended in divorce court was partially due to the separate lives they led. They slept in separate bedrooms. She traveled a lot, and alone, and he had the Room That Didn't Exist, Room 100, which the desk clerks were under strict orders never to book, in case Mr. S. or his friends should want it for privacy.

While this soap opera played itself out, drinks were served in the Polo Lounge, guests found perfect red roses on their room service trays, and people clamored to make reservations. The Pink Palace would survive and flourish, no matter what the turmoil in the executive offices and rooms.

chapter seven

During the years of Ben Silberstein's reign, the legend grew. Hollywood liked to hang out there. It was where you met your friends for lunch or drinks. Grace Kelly and Prince Rainier would throw small, informal cocktail parties in their bungalow, with the princess opening the door for guests. It was where romances began, weddings were celebrated, and a drunken George C. Scott angrily chased Ava Gardner down the hallway in one of many battles in their stormy affair.

Elizabeth Taylor was always checking in and out of the hotel, changing her choice of bungalows as she changed husbands. At one point, management fretted it would run out of bungalows if she didn't stop tying the knot so often.

Marilyn Monroe was often in residence. In fact, Hollywood got some of its earliest glimpses of her at the hotel. Columnist Radie Harris, in her book *Radie's World*, described a dinner dance thrown in 1950 for Vivien Leigh and Laurence Olivier by Sylvia and Danny Kaye. Harris was at a table with Norman Krasna (who wrote *Fury* and *Princess O'Rourke*), Groucho Marx, Eddie Cantor, and agent Johnny Hyde. Harris described Hyde's date as "a very beautiful blond [who] didn't open her mouth the entire evening. This was understandable. Unlike Eddie, Groucho and Norman, this poor bewildered child could hardly expect to contribute much to a conversation full of inside gags and funny asides." Later in the evening, Errol Flynn stopped at the table. "Errol, with his never-failing eye for a beautiful doll, stared at the unfamiliar face next to Johnny Hyde.

"I made the introduction. 'Errol, meet Marilyn Monroe.'

"I don't know if anyone got around to introducing Marilyn to Laurence Olivier on that eventful evening, but if anyone had told her that seven years later Larry would be working for *her* company as *her* costar in *The Prince and the Pauper*...Marilyn would have thought he was pulling her leg."

At another Crystal Room party in the early fifties, Sheilah Graham was with her boss. "John has always had an eye for blondes, and he suddenly pointed to a fair head in the far distance...and demanded, 'Who's that?' 'Oh, a new starlet,' I said. Would he like to meet her? He would. 'You are very pretty ,' he told [the starlet] and predicted 'You will be a great success.'" It was Marilyn, of course.

Little wonder that when President Sukarno of Indonesia saw her in the Polo Lounge and found out who she was, he promptly checked out of the Ambassador and moved over to the Beverly Hills.

It was convenient for Monroe and her husband, playwright Arthur Miller, to stay at the hotel in 1959 when Monroe was set to make a movie for 20th Century-Fox. Gone were the desperate-to-be-noticed starlet days when she had lounged around the pool hoping for the Big Break, made the party scene in the ballrooms, had herself paged in the Polo Lounge, and wiggled through the lobby. She was at the height of her career, with more than twenty-five films under her belt, including the critically acclaimed *Some Like Hot*, which was released that year.

Monroe and Miller were in a bungalow, at the back of the garden, next to one shared by Monroe's costar Yves Montand and his wife, actress Simone Signoret. (Actually Bungalows 20 and 21 are suites on the second floor of a two-story building.)

Montand was a major star in Europe and was hoping this film, *Let's Make Love*, would catapult him into American stardom. He had started out a music-hall man and had been Edith Piaf's protege and lover.

The two couples, unalike as they were, got along. Monroe and Montand would go off to the 20th Century lot early in the morning. Miller would have coffee with the intelligent, literate Signoret, often discussing his day's work schedule with her.

In the evening, after shooting, the four would get together for an unwinding drink and sometimes for dinner. Once Marilyn and Signoret pooled utensils from their kitchenettes and produced a spaghetti meal.

When Monroe had time off, she gravitated to Signoret, a woman she couldn't help admiring. Monroe had been told so often that she was a body with no talent. Signoret, on the other hand, was a recognized actress. The odds were that the French actress would get an Academy Award nomination that year for *Room at the Top*. As it turned out, she was not only nominated, she won Best Actress, as well.

Monroe and Signoret went shopping together and even when to the same colorist to have their hair dyed—a little old lady who claimed to have bleached Jean Harlow's hair.

Then Signoret left. She went to Italy to film *Adua et Ses Compagnes*.

Then Miller left.

Montand, who had counted so much on this picture, was becoming increasingly frustrated as his role was chipped, scraped, and reduced. As more lines were taken from him, he became more morose. A ladies' man, he sought comfort in the arms of his costar. Soon he and Monroe had moved into Bungalow 5.

Montand and Monroe had their affair.

All remained romantic and idyllic until the filming started to wrap up. It then became clear to Monroe that her lover had no intentions of leaving his wife. Montand had lots of affairs. They ended. His marriage did not.

The fights began. One night Monroe locked Montand out of the bungalow. Taking exception to the eviction, he banged on the door, finally breaking it down. She, meanwhile, had called the police. When it was over, explanations made, hushing up done, Montand moved into another bungalow.

It wasn't over for Marilyn. She started her calls. She had to talk to him, the switchboard must put her through. He left instructions they should not. He didn't want to talk to her. The operators felt sorry for Monroe. It was all so sad.

Before Montand was able to make his escape from Southern California, he got a visit from columnist Hedda Hopper, who after years of peeping into others' lives felt qualified to hand out advice on how to live them.

Signoret, in her autobiography, disputed Hopper's version of what ensued. Montand, she contended, didn't speak English well enough to have said what Hopper claims.

"It can't be true," Signoret wrote, "if for no other reason than by its grammatical form and its difficulties of pronunciation it would cost Montand a week's hard work."

As Hopper tells it, she went swooping down on Montand at his bungalow, like an indignant angel. As he invited her in, the phone rang.

"No," he told the operator, "I still won't speak to her. I won't take the call."

"Why not?" Hopper demanded. "You'll probably never see her again. Go on. Speak to her."

He wouldn't. So between sips of her martini, Hopper scolded him. Didn't Montand know that Monroe was "unsophisticated," an innocent? How could you lead her down this primrose path? How could you be so cruel?

"Had Monroe been sophisticated," Montand was supposed to have answered, "none of this ever would have happened. I did everything I could for her when I realized mine was a very small part. The only thing I could stand out in my performance were my love scenes. So, naturally, I did everything I could to make them good! . . . Perhaps she had a schoolgirl's crush. If she did, I'm sorry. But nothing will break up my marriage."

The same could not be said for Monroe's. She and Miller were divorced soon after. Signoret refused to ever stay in Bungalow 5; in fact, she would make an unpleasant gesture whenever she passed it.

Let's Make Love was a bomb, although some critics liked the love scenes.

The staff of the hotel had been aware of problems in the Monroe-Miller marriage even before Montand came on the scene. The author of *View From the Bridge* was out of town when Marilyn went to the Polo Lounge for a drink. She got into a conversation with a man at the next table, who casually mentioned that his wife had yet to arrive. The man returned to his bungalow and was getting ready for bed when he heard a knock on the door. It was Marilyn. She wanted to show him what she wearing under her fur coat and see what he thought of it, would he mind? Before he could answer, she opened the coat. As it turned out, he and many other American men had thought a great deal about what she was wearing underneath. She was wearing nothing.

"What could I do?" he later asked a friend. "I'm a man, after all, I invited her in."

The staff at a hotel, and especially one so geared for service, knows a lot about what goes on behind closed doors, not only with people whose names appear on the entertainment pages. Sometimes they are familiar to those who read the society columns.

Prentis Cobb Hale and his wife, Marialice, could afford to be social butterflies. He was a Hale of the lucrative Broadway-Hale chain of department stores. They were prominent San Francisco Opera Association types.

When they extended their socializing to Los Angeles, the Beverly Hills Hotel was where they stayed. For one thing it was so convenient to their good friend, Denise Minnelli's house.

Denise, a tiny wisp of a woman, was, as someone who knew her put it, a real "climber." She used her address and her former marriage to Vincente Minnelli in her attempts to scale the social ladder.

Denise was always throwing parties and soirees and always looking for guests. She'd show up at the front desk with invitations to be sorted into the mailboxes. She didn't have to know everyone she invited. And if she happened to overlook someone she deemed important—someone like society columnist Suzy—Denise would scurry across the street in the middle of the night, dressed in nightgown and sunglasses, to make sure the important person got an invitation.

Physically they were an odd triangle. Prentis was robust, a boisterous fellow who looked as if he might at any moment leap into his jodhpurs and be off chasing the hounds. Marialice was big and matronly. Her clothes never hung quite the way the designer intended. Standing next to Marialice, Denise looked even smaller and more delicate than she was. They were such good friends.

There came a night when Prentis left for a Denise party, but his wife stayed in the hotel. A room service waiter, on his way back to the kitchen, heard someone weeping and decided to investigate.

The sobs were from Mrs. Hale. She was hunched over on the steps outside her bungalow.

"What's wrong, Mrs. Hale? Is there something I can do, something I can get you?" The waiter was concerned. This was a woman he had waited on and chatted with for years. Not a friend, in any real sense, but a guest, his guest, and a person in distress.

"If only there were. There's nothing I can do. I've tried," Mrs. Hale wept.

The waiter didn't know what she was talking about, but it was clear she needed to unburden herself to someone.

"It's that awful woman. She's stealing my husband. What am I to do?"

There was nothing she could do on the bungalow steps, the waiter said, trying to soothe her. Go inside. Lie down. Perhaps in the morning . . .

It wasn't long before Denise threw another party, this time in celebration of Mrs. Hale's birthday.

Prentis went. Marialice didn't.

On March 26, 1969, the headline in the *San Francisco Chronicle* read, *MRS. PRENTIS COBB HALE KILLS HERSELF*.

It happened in the family mansion. She shot herself, one .38-caliber bullet, directly through the head.

Prentis had spoken to her as she got ready for bed. Then he went downstairs to watch television.

"I heard one shot," he said. He raced upstairs, and there she was on the floor of his dressing room.

She had, he said, given no indication she would take her life.

Not long afterward, Denise Minnelli changed her name to Mrs. Prentis Cobb Hale.

While much of a romantic and marital nature occurred at the hotel during these years, it was also a hub for movie-making deals, drawing the most familiar names in show business, along with those who wished to become so. Bungalows and suites were homes to the east coast moneymen out to check on their investments. It was where movie projects started, actors auditioned, and the stars were interviewed and interviewed and interviewed.

Vincente Minnelli worked out the details of many of his pictures, including *Gigi* and *An American in Paris*, in the Polo Lounge. When Frank Capra's *Pocketful of Miracles* got high audience ratings at sneak previews, studio president Arthur Krim called a strategy meeting in his bungalow to brainstorm the best way and time to release what they were sure would be a big-box office hit. Arthur Miller persuaded Clark Gable to appear in *The Misfits*, a movie Miller had written. Gable was not sure he understood the character of the modern cowboy Miller wanted him to portray, but in the end he agreed. It was Gable's last picture. Many believed the physically strenuous role and having to wait in blistering heat for an always-tardy Marilyn Monroe contributed to Gable's death at the end of the film's production.

Ann-Margret huddled with her husband Roger Smith and agent Alan Carr day after day trying to decide what to do with her career, which wasn't going much beyond roles as Elvis Presley's love interest. The talks led to her becoming one of Las Vegas' highest-paid entertainers as well as receiving an Academy nomination for *Carnal Knowledge*.

Charles Bludhorn bought Paramount Pictues for Gulf and Western at a table in the Polo Lounge. The Polo Lounge at breakfast—actually it was the Loggia and Patio, the Polo Lounge is technically only the dark inside cocktail area, with the gold-leaf mural of ancient Persian polo players over the bar—was a mecca for deal making. Literary agents touted manuscripts to east coast publishers. Producers wove storylines for backers. Investors used the pink phones that were brought to tables to call their New York brokers with buy-and-sell orders. The hostess, Bernice Philbin and her ten waitresses would make sure that the easterners got out in time to make the 9 o'clock flight to New York.

(Peter Finch was on his way to the Loggia for a breakfast conference with *Network* director Sidney Lumet when he collapsed in the lobby and died.)

At lunchtime the crew and the atmosphere changed. The host was Nino Osti—he later moved to the night shift—and the favored place was the Patio, still shaded by the Brazilian pepper tree planted by Hernando Courtright.

There was more socializing and less business at lunch, but invariably some reporter would be scarfing a free meal while interviewing an actor or director and occasionally a producer looking to plug a new film. You'd see Raymond Massey congratulating Burgess Meredith on his Oscar nomination for *Rocky,* while United Press International writer Vernon Scott scribbled notes. If you wanted to find the heart of Hollywood, the Polo Lounge and its satellites were the place.

In the seventies, an Englishman lamented that he had been disappointed with his visit to Los Angeles. Not once did he get to stand behind Barbra Streisand in the supermarket or purchase Band-Aids next to Charlton Heston in Thrifty Drugs. After weeks of peering into windows of Rolls-Royces waiting at traffic lights next to him, he had not seen one Star.

One day he happened into the Beverly Hills Hotel where he saw someone who looked "incredibly" like Michael Caine at the bar. The visitor wandered over to a phone and, as he later reported, "it occurred to me that the man already occupying the booth was Warren Beatty, and I was about to remark this to the character in front of me, when I realized the character in front of me was Ringo Starr. I was suddenly overwhelmed by the fact that this place wasn't a myth, but actually real."

There was action at the pool. Walter Winchell, in his loud staccato delivery, used the phone there to call in his columns. Mark Goodson, the TV game producer, lived part of the year at the hotel and was thought to be the most paged man at the pool. "Calling Mark Goodson. Calling Mark Goodson." He was there when the pool opened at 10 a.m. and was still around when it closed at 7:30, with a secretary and two telephones. He would be joined by industrialist Norton Simon, who worked at waterside as well. It is believed that Leonard Bernstein came up with the idea for *West Side Story* there. Supposedly he was working on the Romeo-Juliet theme using Jewish and Irish protagonists (a musical *Lennie's Irish Rose*) then changed his mind and went with warring Hispanic-Caucasion gangs.

The story of Bob Evans, later husband of Ali McGraw and a powerful producer, was not legend. Mike Silverman, something of a legend himself in Beverly Hills real estate, was at the pool the day Norma Shearer was discussing casting *The Man of a Thousand Faces*, a biomovie of her late husband, MGM executive Irving Thalberg. Talking about actors to play Thalberg, she glanced across the pool and asked, "Who's that nice-looking man? He has a strong resemblance to my husband."

The nice-looking man was Evans, who with his brother, Charles, owned the clothing firm of Evan-Picone. Bob Evans used to visit the hotel to "troll for starlets," as Silverman puts it. He was signed for the lead in the Thalberg movie, got savage reviews, appeared in several more films (including *The Fiend Who Walked the West* in which he had the title role), and then mercifully switched his efforts to behind the camera.

The business Jacqueline *Valley of the Dolls* Susann did at the Beverly Hills was write her best sellers. She would borrow a big blackboard from the kitchen to keep track of her characters and plotlines. She was charming and friendly, a genuine favorite of the staff, which was unaware she was suffering from cancer. Sven Petersen, the pool manager, was even included by name in *Once Is Not Enough.*

In a book about his late wife, Irving Mansfield told of Jackie deciding to have a quiet dinner with him and Rex Reed, instead of attending a party. The next morning at the pool, Johnny Carson came over to ask them "Have you heard what happened? Isn't it awful? A maniac got loose at Sharon Tate's house last night. He killed Sharon and several others." Tate, who had starred in the movie version of *Valley,* had literally been slaughtered. Police later arrested Charles Manson and some of his "family" members for the murders. Susann went into shock—the party she had chosen not to attend had been at Sharon Tate's house.

Over these years, the hotel had more than its share of eccentric guests.

Miss Prell would have to be counted as one of them. Twice a week she would leave for her walk to the post office. One step, two. She sidled down the staircase, her back pressed to the wall.

The Hertz rent-a-car girls would be the first to see her coming and, as usual, tried to suppress their giggles, but it was hard. Miss Prell was so . . . well, so comical, with her dyed red hair, her toreador pants and halter tops, and her bright red lipstick, which covered not only her lips, but half her gaunt face as well.

One step, two. Miss Prell made it to the lobby floor. The low buzz would stop as people gawked at the apparition scuttling toward the door.

"Hello, Miss Prell," someone in the cashier's cage would call.

"Oh! Oh!" answered Miss Prell as she hurried out.

One hour later - six blocks there, six blocks back—Miss Prell reversed her scuttle, up the stairs, back pressed to wall, a fast feint past the Hertz counter, down the hall to room 236.

Miss Prell was home safe again.

Miss Ruth Prell has been at the Beverly Hills since the forties. The inheritance from her family's shampoo fortune enabled her to live year-round at the hotel and give some of the employees gift subscriptions to the *Christian Science Monitor* at Christmastime. She only left the hotel three times a week, twice to the post office and once on Sunday to attend Christian Science services.

At one time, Miss Prell shared a room with her sister, Mrs. Ethel Brown, who was more outgoing and not as strange. The two had attended their Christian Science meetings together and had been looked upon with good-natured tolerance. Ethel would chat with the maids once in a while, or the desk clerks, inquiring about who was in the hotel, like a schoolgirl about to read *Photoplay*.

Then Ethel began feeling poorly. It was tuberculosis, but being a Christian Scientist, she refused to put herself under a doctor's care.

The maids were concerned—Mrs. Brown was so nice—but there was nothing they could do. The two sisters knew what they were about, and that was that. One day, Ethel was worse than usual. She didn't even get out of bed when the maid came to tidy up. The cleaning was done quickly and quietly so as not to awaken her. The maid left with a nod to Miss Prell, who was sitting quietly in one of the overstuffed chairs.

"I hope Mrs. Brown is feeling better tomorrow," the maid whispered.

Ethel wasn't any better the second day. She was still in bed, eyes closed. Miss Prell was still sitting quietly in her chair.

The third day, Ethel was still sleeping. While dusting, the curious maid inched over to the bed to get a better look.

"Miss Prell," she called, alarmed, "Something may be wrong. Mrs. Brown isn't moving."

"Oh, I wouldn't think so," said the unperturbed Miss Prell. "She passed on two days ago."

But no one, *NO ONE*, could ever match the strangeness and odd behavior of another of the hotel's longtime guests.

Howard Robard Hughes, one of the richest men in the world, if not the richest. Hughes had started amassing his wealth in 1923 at the age of nineteen. That was the year his father died leaving him the majority interest in the Hughes Tool Company, which held the patent on an oil and gas drilling bit needed at almost every well around the world.

Hughes parlayed this inheritance, which was worth approximately $871,000, into $2 billion before his death in 1976. Along the way, he owned a movie studio, controlled an airline, flew airplanes, dated some of the most beautiful women in Hollywood—including Ava Gardner, Katharine Hepburn, and Jean Harlow—designed a bra for Jane Russell, and lived at the Beverly Hills Hotel.

For almost thirty years Howard Hughes made the hotel his home, or at least one of his homes. By the 1950s and into the sixties Hughes had no fewer than four bungalows, two suites, and two rooms on a daily, year-round, no-discount basis, at a cost of more than a thousand dollars a day. (Some sources put the number of bungalows at seven.) He would have taken more, only the manager politely but firmly said no.

After his marriage to Jean Peters in 1957, he occupied a four-room bungalow, and she stayed in one with three rooms on the other side of the hotel grounds. A third bungalow and some of the rooms were for his eight Mormon bodyguards; the suites he kept for any guests he might have.

Once real estate man Mike Silverman—who is said to resemble Cary Grant—found wine writer Robert Balzer sitting at the hotel pool, looking bewildered and depressed.

When Silverman asked what was bothering him, Balzer explained that he had been trying to lease his house in the hills above Los Angeles for $10,000 a month with no success. Then he got a call from someone who did not identify himself.

The caller wanted to lease the house for five months—and would pay double what Balzer was asking, $20,000 per month. There were conditions, however. Balzer was to leave the house within the hour, check into the Beverly Hills Hotel, and make no effort to return to his house for the duration of the lease. "But what about my clothes?" Balzer had asked. "What if I need more clothes?" "Go to the men's store at the hotel, pick out anything you want or need, and charge it to this account." Balzer was given a store-account number.

Even though it was weird, the offer was too good to turn down. So there Balzer sat, disoriented and worried about what he had gotten himself into.

Silverman, who likes to know what's going on in town, especially when it comes to real estate, drove up to Balzer's house, only to be turned back by a security guard. He later learned the leasee was Hughes, in a hurry to secure some place to stash his latest girlfriend. Balzer, then, was one of those "guests" put in the extra suites, all because his house fit Hughes's requirements for something big with high walls and privacy.

One bungalow that Hughes rented was left completely empty. No one was allowed in, not even maintenance men. One bellboy, perhaps emboldened because he was there only for his summer vacation, did sneak a peek. He could see deep layers of dust sitting on piles and piles of records, engineering reports, specifications—and the blueprints for the Spruce Goose. The Goose was the transport plane, the flying boat, Hughes had designed to help win World War II.

It wasn't ready for test-flying until 1947 and then managed to get up only seventy feet and fly just one mile. Hughes was injured in the crash and had trouble hearing afterwards. Some believed that the accident triggered his descent into madness. Towards the end of his life, when he had gone into seclusion, his top aide, Robert Maheu, who never met him, would receive memos bordering on the insane. "There were times in his last years that he was void of reality... There were some memos where references pertaining to absolute power were sent to me. To protect him from himself, I took no action on these memos. To buy a particular president or to buy someone into the White House ..."

The empty bungalow caused problems for the plumbing in all the bungalows. Since no plumbers were allowed in, the pipelines to the building eventually corroded. These lines crossed with others, and after a while all the plumbing was acting up.

In the midfifties Hughes went to great lengths to avoid being seen, in contrast to the twenties when he was the young man about Hollywood and would cruise around in a Dusenberg or any number of other flamboyant cars he owned. Now he would hide in a panel truck disguised as a butcher's van making deliveries. Management honored his insistence on privacy. It was forbidden for the staff to acknowledge he was there. Despite that, people found out.

Nan Kirsch, who was to later marry *Los Angeles Times* book reviewer Robert Kirsch, remembered going to the Polo Lounge with friends when she was still below the drinking age. It was fun to see whether any of the men would notice her and, even if they didn't, it was so sophisticated to sip on a pina colada or some other grown-up drink.

Once on her way back from the ladies' room, she got turned around and started heading down an unfamiliar hallway. She hadn't gone far when a a hand shot out of a shadow and grabbed her shoulder.

"Miss," the owner of the hand said, "no one is allowed down this corridor. Go back the way you came."

It was spooky, just like in the movies. She went back much faster than she had come. Safely seated at her little round table in the sanctuary of the Polo Lounge, she asked the waiter what the big deal was down that corridor.

"Oh," he said, lowering his voice out of habit, "those are Mr. Hughes's rooms. No one goes there."

Hughes was obsessive about privacy and security. He would walk away from million dollar deals if he heard the buyer had so much as talked to a bank about financing. Once he called the front desk at 3:30 a.m. wanting to book the Crystal Room for a conference. This room could accommodate up to 750 people for a meeting and 1,000 for a cocktail party or reception.

"How many people will be attending your conference?" the clerk asked.

Well, there would be three—no, there would be four, counting Hughes.

"But, Mr. Hughes," the clerk sputtered, "wouldn't you prefer a smaller room? Surely a smaller room would fit your needs."

No, Hughes was adamant that he needed the Crystal Room, and furthermore, he needed it in half an hour. (Hughes had never been one to stand on convention when renting public spaces at the hotel. When he was younger, he would hire the orchestra in the hotel's Persian Room to play all night. He had insomnia.)

So it was that at 4:00 that morning, Hughes and his fellow conferees sat down at a small round table that had been placed under the large center chandelier. Hughes later confided to the manager that it was one of the few times he felt completely secure at a meeting. By being so far from doors and walls, no prying ears or listening devices could have possibly picked up the conversation.

While the venue of the meeting was out of the ordinary, the time was not. Hughes was a night person and usually held meetings when other people were long since in bed—as Henry Crown discovered.

In 1961 the Crown family was one of the richest in the country, with many real estate properties (including six coal mines) and major holdings in such firms as General Dynamics, Pennzoil, Rock Island Railroad, and Aetna Life and Casualty.

Crown was having dinner at the home of some friends in Beverly Hills when the butler announced he had a call.

"But it can't be for me. Nobody knows I'm here. Besides, the phone number here is unlisted, isn't it?"

Curious, he took the call and found himself talking to Howard Hughes. Would Mr. Crown be available to discuss a business proposal with Hughes later that evening when Crown returned to his hotel (not the Beverly Hills).

Even if Hughes didn't own and control TWA, General Dynamics' biggest civilian customer, Crown would have agreed. Hughes had become a mysterious figure, the bashful billionaire.

Hughes didn't get around to calling until the next morning. Without bothering to apologize for keeping Crown sitting by the phone for hours, Hughes launched into his proposition. TWA needed $250 million right away to keep from crashing into bankruptcy. Although Hughes was worth $750 million, the money was tied up in Hughes Tools and TWA. The Crown family had no similar cash-flow inconveniences.

According to the *New York Times*, Hughes sketched out the following plan: "Mr. Crown would lend Mr. Hughes $50 million, borrowed from the Bank of America using the Empire State Building as collateral. If this took place, the bank had agreed to lend another $50 million directly to Mr. Hughes. That $100 million would provide the financial underpinning that would enable Mr. Hughes to sell $150 million in securities."

With the fate of General Dynamics so tied to TWA's, Crown was more than interested in helping out Hughes and agreed to meet him at his Beverly Hills Hotel bungalow. But not during the day, no, this was Howard Hughes with whom he was dealing. It would have to be at night. So it was that Crown found himself walking through the hotel gardens in darkness, headed towards Hughes' bungalow. He stopped short when he heard his name whispered. Looking around, he realized there was a tall man shadowed under a nearby palm. It was Hughes. He motioned Crown over to the tree, where he and Hughes, two of America's wealthiest men, agreed to the multimillion dollar deal.

Crown left thinking that as long as his accountants found Hughes' empire solid, all that was left was for the papers to be drawn up and signed. The papers were drawn up and taken over for Hughes's signature by officials of the Bank of America. They were met at the bungalow door by Mormon bodyguards. "Mr. Hughes is quite sick now," the officials were told. "He is too weak to sign his name."

Hughes ended up bailing out of TWA and selling his stock for $85 a share, coming away with $550 million for himself.

Almost twenty years earlier, another executive interested in doing business with Hughes actually got inside the bungalow. Naturally, it was late at night when the man was allowed in to discuss the possible purchase of Hughes Tool. It was hard to pay attention, however, when he found himself facing sketches of Jane Russell in various brassieres. Hughes was working with the studio art director and wardrobe girl to design a bra that would do the most justice to Russell's best attributes.

In 1951 Sheilah Graham had her strange interlude with Hughes at the hotel. Graham had the flu, but he insisted he had to see her. He had a scoop for her. A big scoop.

As Albert B. Gerber tells it in his book, *Bashful Billionaire* (the first book published about Hughes because he paid off authors not to write about him):

"Ten minutes later a car arrived to pick her up. The chauffeur took her on a circuitous route which lasted more than thirty minutes. It had, by now, grown dark and Miss Graham could not identify her whereabouts any longer. Finally the car drew up at what appeared to be the back entrance of a one-story bungalow. From the shrubbery, the garbage cans and the enormous Spanish building outlined against the sky, she recognized she was at the back entrance of a Beverly Hills Hotel bungalow. Since the hotel was at most a three minute drive from her home, she concluded that the drive had been intended to confuse her."

And the Scoop?

Howard Hughes wanted to make sure that Sheilah Graham knew Elizabeth Taylor's latest boyfriend, a man who held a high position in the film world, was a *Communist*.

Graham, who had different ideas on what constituted a big story, thanked Mr. Hughes for his information and left.

Hughes was a rabid Communist-baiter. And his role in the tragedy of the Hollywood blacklistings is often overlooked. He fired Dore Schary from RKO because Hughes believed him a leftist sympathizer.

Perhaps a fear that one of the "pinkos" he destroyed was out to get him led Hughes to hire a food taster. Hughes also put Garry Reich, the hotel's head chef, on his payroll. No matter where in the world Hughes was, he insisted that Reich send him one meal a day. It is unclear when Reich, who continued his regular duties at the hotel, started cooking for Hughes. It was probably after the bizarre phone call the kitchen got one evening from Hughes asking to speak to the chef.

"This is Howard Hughes's bungalow. I want you to prepare this order personally. You personally, no one else."

Hughes then asked for two roast beef sandwiches, to be wrapped in waxed paper. The chef was to deliver them personally, at exactly 6 p.m., on a tray, placed in the forked tree outside the bungalow. Hughes further instructed the chef not to look around or wait. Put the tray in the fork of the tree and leave. The chef was to deliver the same order in the same manner every day at the same time, understood?

It sounded simple enough. At precisely six, the tray and sandwiches were put precisely where Hughes wanted them. The next evening, the chef returned with two more sandwiches only to find the ones from the day before still in the tree untouched. The chef was puzzled but did as he had been told and replaced the stale sandwiches with the fresh ones.

On third day, the chef again went out with sandwiches at the requested time and again the tray was untouched. This time he decided he must have misheard Hughes and left nothing in the tree. No sooner had the chef gotten back to the kitchen than the phone rang.

"This is Howard Hughes. Where is my order?"

The kitchen dealt with other Hughes quirks like his craving for upside-down cake, which he would want in the middle of the night. Then there were his kadota fig orders. A serving normally contained twelve figs. Hughes would order twenty-three. If twenty-four were inadvertently given to him, he sent the figs back.

Hughes always ate in his bungalow, and Peters always ate in hers, which didn't mean they ate separately. During dinner they were on the phone with each other, carrying on polite conversation as if they were at the same table.

It wasn't until after Hughes moved to Las Vegas and had released all his rooms at the hotel that Reich was dropped from his payroll. Reich, who was very good and deserved every penny he got, went to Silberstein and Slatkin and asked for a raise, now that he had lost his supplemental income. Even though the hotel was doing very well and the Crystal Room and restaurants under Reich's supervision were bringing in lots of money, he was turned down. Reich quit. First he went to the Los Angeles Country Club and then to a job he couldn't turn down—Disney World. Reich was put in charge of all the food in the vast complex, from the ice cream stands on Main Street to the executives' private dining rooms.

The irony was that Slatkin and Silberstein had to pay the succession of chefs that followed Reich far more than he had asked.

An automobile leasing company was another loser when Hughes left California. Besides the "meat" truck mentioned earlier, Hughes kept a 1932 Chevrolet that he allowed no one else to drive. Peters would often show up in a chauffeur-driven station wagon.

In early years, Hughes hired limousines from a prestigious Beverly Hills car agency. One of the drivers was an elderly black gentleman. One day the driver timidly handed Hughes his personal business card and told him that he had fine old Cadillac for hire, if Hughes would prefer it to the agency's. Hughes grunted and shoved the card into his pocket. Months later the driver got a call from the Hughes people. Mr. Hughes wanted to rent his limousine for one day and one day only. The driver had hoped for something longer, but a rental was a rental, so he drove the limousine to the street outside Hughes's bungalow. He was met by one of Hughes's men who told him to leave the car and come back for it the next day.

When the driver returned, he was told Hughes wanted the Cadillac for an additional day. This repeated itself day after day. The old driver would show up for the car only to be told Hughes still needed it. Every so often, the driver would start up the car, check its transmission, and polish it. Finally one evening, after many months, the driver received an urgent call. Mr. Hughes no longer wanted the car, and it should be picked up the next morning. The driver had made so much money from Hughes paying a daily rental rate that he was able to quit his job at the agency, buy a small fleet of used Cadillacs, and go into business himself.

Hughes invariably kept two or three cars parked around the hotel, waiting, with full gas tanks filled, for when, if ever, Hughes decided to use them.

He also kept two leased Cadillacs in the garage. They were never moved; they just sat there with their tires flat.

Year after year Hughes paid the leasing company for the privilege of the cars' disuse. He would tip the garagemen six hundred dollars at Christmas for doing nothing but keep his cars in nonworking order.

With his rooms, Hughes gave up the garage space, and the leasing company—not to mention the garage guys—lost their free ride.

After Hughes died, thirty-five "lost" wills came out of the woodwork. One, that surfaced in 1981, was purported to have been written in 1960. It looked authentic. It had been typed on a 1956 IBM Courier on Beverly Hills Hotel stationery of the period. This will, like the others, was a hoax. Unlike the others, the man behind the fraud, Harold W. Mallet, a vice-president of Aspen Airlines, earned an historical footnote by being the only person convicted of fabricating a Hughes will. He pleaded no contest to perjury and grand theft conspiracy charges.

That the hotel could easily absorb the demands and peculiarities of its eccentrics without other guests being inconvenienced was due in part to its rambling layout—sixteen acres, twenty-one bungalows, and two-hundred-and-sixty-five rooms. Greater credit went to the staff. There was a remarkable group of people working at the hotel during this period, intent on providing remarkable service. Some were better than others; some nicer or more interesting; some like Sven, at the pool, became something of celebrities about whom stories were written; but the thing that counted was they worked together to give the hotel the character and charm that it had.

One of the first staff members a guest had contact with was Hollis Polodna, the reservations manager whose signature appeared at the bottom of confirmation letters.

Polodna was the man who thoughtfully assigned Margaret Truman, on her 1972 visit, the same room she had occupied in 1950, when, as First Daughter, she sang in the Hollywood Bowl. Because of his power in assigning rooms, Polodna was a well-tipped man.

Bill Bixby, the assistant reservation manager, would never take a tip handed directly over the counter, but guests found a way to keep him in Guccis.

Manning the front desk during the day was Nick Pappas, an assistant manager. After a rough divorce, he lived for a time in one of the hotel's smallest rooms, free of charge. Nor did Pappas have to pay for meals. Silberstein wouldn't let him because Silberstein could sympathize with rough divorces.

At night there was Ernie Brown, a sweet gem of a man who started working at the hotel in the early fifties. There were no problems he couldn't handle and no lengths to which he wouldn't go for a guest.

Take the time the German baroness, a member of the Krupp armaments family, was missing a bag. Without much concern or anxiety, she explained to Brown that the airline had misplaced it. Ordinarily, the baroness said, she wouldn't have bothered Brown with such a trivial matter but, well, "I have all my jewelry in that bag. I forgot to carry it as I usually do and put it in the suitcase. I've never lost a suitcase before."

Just how much jewelry was she talking about? Three million dollars worth. Somewhere, in some city serviced by the airline, was the baroness's three million dollars' worth of jewels.

Brown raced to the airport and spent most the night having a trace put on the bag. Miraculously, it turned up in Rio de Janeiro and was quickly returned to the baroness.

Other staff members would go to Ernie Brown if there was something they couldn't handle. In the case of Nino Osti, it was the Scotchman who came into the Polo Lounge one night. After being served, the man was presented with a check for forty-eight dollars.

When the waiter came for payment, the Scotchman handed him forty. "Sir," the waiter said, "I think you've made a mistake. The check is for forty-eight." In a heavy Scottish burr, he announced, "I've eaten in restaurants all over the world, and I'm telling you what you gave me was worth forty dollars and that's all I'm going to pay."

The waiter retreated for reinforcements and returned with Osti. In his mellifluous voice still flavored with strong echoes of his native Milan, Osti tried to reason with the guest. "Sir, you were given a menu. You knew the prices when you ordered. See, the bill is forty-eight dollars."

Stubbornly the Scotchman repeated that he'd eaten everywhere and his meal was worth only forty dollars.

In desperation, Nino sent for Ernie Brown. After being briefed on the situation, Brown went to the Scotchman's table and said in a reasonable tone, "I understand, sir, you don't want to pay the full amount of your bill. That is up to you. But I should inform you ..." Brown's tone of voice didn't change. "... that as soon as you step out of the hotel lobby, there will be several Beverly Hills policemen waiting to arrest you."

The Scotchman studied Brown's face for a second to see if he were serious, then quickly paid the bill—all forty-eight dollars worth.

Brown was often assisted at the front desk by his black, silver-flecked standard poodle, Tina. For many years pets were welcome at the hotel. For an extra five dollars a night, you could bring your dog or cat. The animals did have to register on their own little guest cards, although paw prints weren't required.

Elizabeth Taylor often brought her dogs. When she was married to Eddie Fisher, she had some that weren't completely housebroken. Occasionally they would even wet the beds. The smell became so bad that the mattress had to be thrown out. (Taylor's studio was charged for a new one.)

The pet policy was a great convenience for someone like Liza Minnelli. When her house was being painted, she and her two cats checked into the hotel to escape the fumes.

The Duke and Duchess of Windsor brought their pugs. The ugly little dogs almost caused a revolt in the kitchen when the chef discovered the steak filets he was preparing with such care each night were not for the duke and duchess, but for their dogs. (The pugs had their own sitter when their masters stepped out for the evening.)

Special puppyburgers could be ordered from room service. A mixture of ground beef, carrots, and peas, they cost three dollars and were supposed to be quite tasty, even if you weren't a dog.

The Pets-Are-Welcome policy did not extend to bear cubs, but that didn't stop the fourteen-year-old son of Ali Ipar of Turkey from sneaking one into his room. For several days, he kept it hidden in the bathroom without the maids discovering it. Room service, on the other hand, got suspicious of the strange—even for a fourteen-year old—orders it kept getting. They conveyed their suspicions to the front desk and a surreptitious inspection was made. It must have been a shock finding a bear in the bathroom, but calm prevailed, and the cub was evicted.

By the end of the seventies, the welcome sign for pets had been taken down. There were some guests who had abused the courtesy. Robert de Niro had shown up with seven cats to keep him company while filming the disastrous *The Last Tycoon*.

After the ban went into effect, a New York book publisher, not known for following rules, could not understand how anyone would object to his tiny toy poodle, Cinnamon. Besides, it was easy enough to smuggle the little fur ball along a garden path to his bungalow, which is what he did.

For several days all went smoothly, as Cinnamon frolicked in and around the bungalow. But then the dog must have noticed there were other flowers to smell and new hands to be licked, so off she went in pursuit of adventure—and maybe a treat or two.

When the publisher and his party noticed Cinnamon's absence, a search was launched. Two hours passed and no puppy. Finally she was discovered on a nearby patio, playing with some people from Paris.

After thanking their neighbors for having taken care of the errant pooch, publisher and party were returning to their bungalow when it occurred to seven-year-old Jennifer that it was quite logical for a French poodle to seek out a Parisian couple.

At check-out time, the publisher was relishing the fact he'd put one over on the hotel. Having settled the bill, he was almost to the door when one of the desk clerks called out that it had been very nice seeing him again, adding "And we aren't even going to mention the dog."

Tina, Ernie Brown's dog, was given special dispensation to be in the hotel, since technically she was working and not a guest. Besides her, Brown had two clerks to help him on duty, as all the assistant managers did.

The clerks had a wide range of duties, including typing up information cards on arriving guests, making out another slip in triplicate (one that was immediately plopped down a pneumatic tube to the switchboard so they could address guests by name when putting through calls), and preparing a folio for the cashier's office. Better rooms were assigned by assistant managers and above; parceling out less desirable rooms was left to the clerks. The clerks were also expected to hand out keys, sort mail into boxes, and answer questions and the phone—often the hardest part of the job.

Sometimes the clerks would have to field calls from a drunk Steve McQueen, who was sure that his then-wife Ali McGraw was two-timing him with Warren Beatty. The star of *Love With a Proper Stranger* and *The Thomas Crown Affair* wouldn't believe the clerk when he said McGraw had not been in all evening. "If she's with Mr. Beatty, I would suggest you try the Wilshire. He has a suite there, you know, not here."

"Listen you," McQueen growled, sounding as if he'd like to punch the clerk's lights out, "check the Polo Lounge. Ali always goes to the Polo Lounge when she messes around." McQueen should have known, since that had been her trysting spot with him when she was married to Bob Evans.

If it wasn't McQueen, it might be David Janssen, star of TV's *The Fugitive*. He would call late at night desperate to talk to anyone about anything, the World Series, the weather, anything so long as someone was on the line.

Clerks were also the arbiters of proper attire. Guests would solicit their advice on what to wear.

"Well, I'm going to a cocktail party in the Hills. Do you think it will be terribly formal or do you always dress down out here?"

Wives without husbands would call for help in buttoning buttons, and husbands without wives were invariably in need of assistance with their ties.

"I must have tied a thousand ties," says one former clerk. "Guys who have no idea how to tie a tie because their wives always do it for them. Incredible."

Simone Signoret had one favorite bellman. "Please, I need help," she'd phone in. "I'm up at some place in the hills, and I don't know how to get back. Would you come and get me?"

Next the clerks' station, around the bend of the front desk, were the cashier's cages. Two cashiers worked per shift with an auditor-cashier taking over at graveyard time.

Some cashiers came and went, and others seemed to stay forever. In the latter category was a sixtyish woman who didn't have to work. Her family had money, allowing her to be casual about such details as working hours. At one time this cashier commandeered four of the hotel's safe-deposit boxes—one for stocks and bonds, another for cash, a third for jewelry, and the last for her insurance policies.

Finally someone worked up enough courage to say, "Gee, I think our guests would like to use a safe—couldn't you give up at least one?"

This cashier had the odd habit of washing her pencils. If she didn't like a particular guest, she stuck a *Closed* sign on her window until the person left.

Any organization is going to have its stars, and the Beverly Hills was no exception. One was Leon Smith, but who knew him by that name? He was Smitty. The tall, uniformed fixture at the end of the porte cochere. A newspaper or magazine article about the hotel wouldn't be complete without mentioning him.

Smitty started parking cars at the hotel when he was sixteen, in 1939.

"I never thought I'd stay," he said, "when I came to park cars at night and work in a service station during the day." In the best Horatio Alger tradition, Smitty went from parking boy to partner and then with some associates to owner of the concession, which is leased from the hotel.

Smitty was a man to be cultivated. His greeting you by name meant extra status points. "The advantage...when we know them is that we get their car quickly without having to ask for a name. But even if they have a Rolls-Royce, we need to know more than 'Get my Rolls.' In the old days that would do, but we have so many now."

Smitty made a lot of money over the years. Reportedly, he paid the car jockeys—four full-time and more than twenty part-time—a straight salary. Any tips had to be handed over to him. One of the part-time jockeys—they were usually college students—took exception to this policy and would stash some of his tips in a hole in a tree. Even without those gratuities, Smitty did very well. There was standing joke that Smitty was the third richest man in Southern California. When he finally sold the concession, he still came back on Saturdays. He couldn't play golf every day, he explained.

Another employee who frequently found his way into print was Buddy Douglas, a midget who had taken the job of pager in the early fifties. He would wander into the lobby and the Polo Lounge yelling, "Ca-ll for Mistah Silvah-man" or "Ca-ll for Carroll O'Conn-ah" in the very same way he used to yell, "Ca-ll for Phil-lip Mo-rris" in commercials. Between Buddy and the cigarette girl who worked the room, it was like being in a movie from the thirties or forties.

Waiter Willie (Pancho) Holquin was a mainstay in the Polo Lounge, having worked there since it opened. Holquin was credited with creating the guacamole. Getting a complimentary tray of guacamole and chips placed on your table without asking for it was a sign that you were somebody in the Polo Lounge. Pancho was the only one exempt from a firm hotel rule against autograph collecting. He was allowed to ask celebrities frequenting the lounge to sign his book. The first page had a sketch of a shooting star done in the style of the signer, Salvador Dali. "To my good friend, Willie," the artist wrote in 1938.

Pancho was always good for Polo Lounge memorabilia—having witnessed much of what was worth remembering.

Mario Lanza quietly drinking white wine in a corner booth and suddenly launching into song. When he was finished, he drank what remained of his wine, and walked out, leaving the other patrons stunned by the beauty of his voice and the timing of his performance.

Frank Sinatra and Dean Martin getting into a brawl with some strangers in 1966.

Press agent Russell Birdwell casually mentioning he was looking for ex-French Foreign Legionnaires for a publicity campaign he was mounting for the movie *Beau Geste* only to be told four were working as waiters in the Polo Lounge. "Can you beat that? Four former legionnaires in one place. Hell, I put them all in the movie." (Part of Birdwell's place in Hollywood lore came from a conversation he had with Marlene Dietrich at the lounge's center booth. Dietrich was complaining about constantly being described as having the most beautiful legs in the world. Birdwell, always looking for a new gimmick, suggested she do the opposite of what was expected of her by wearing pants—hence, he said, the pantsuit was born.)

H. R. Haldeman was in the Polo Lounge when he learned of the bungled break-in at Watergate. Though far more telling was John Mitchell's reaction in his room. He was being served dinner by Bernie Bloch, the peerless head of room service. Bloch had carefully checked the Sterno burner, laid out the silver, filled the water goblet, felt the rolls to make sure they were warm, moved the perfect red rose in its slender ceramic vase to one side so it wouldn't be in the way, pulled out a warmed plate from beneath the serving cart, and set the meal before the jowly, grimmed-faced president's man, John Mitchell, who had been oblivious of the time-honed performance because he was watching the nightly network news.

Mitchell had been attorney general of the United States, but was now Richard Milhous Nixon's campaign manager, director of the Committee for the Re-election of the President—you have to wonder when they realized the committee's acronym was CREEP.

Bloch figured Mitchell was in town to raise more money for the party coffers. Bloch had seen other Nixon big guns, like Haldeman, floating around the lobby. The waiter would have recognized these men without any coaching from Walter Cronkite. They were hundred dollar tippers —which was why, as head of room service, Bloch always waited on John Mitchell.

As he worked, Bloch had caught a snatch or two of the news broadcast.

George McGovern expected to win most of the New York delegates at the Democratic convention.

Heavy bombing in North Vietnam.

Fiddler on the Roof becoming the longest-running show in Broadway history.

It was all Muzak information to Bloch. Then the item came on about some burglary, a break-in at the Democratic National Committee offices, in some place called Watergate. The network news didn't assign it much importance and neither would have Bloch—if not for John Mitchell.

"Son of a bitch!" Mitchell screamed. "Goddamn! They fucked it! They fucked it!"

Mitchell shoved the table away and bellowed for Bloch to "Take the food away. Take everything away. I've got to get to the telephone. Out of the room!"

That was June 17, 1972. On June 18, a more-composed John Mitchell told the world that the Watergate burglars "were not operating on either our [CREEP's] behalf or with our consent. There is no place in our campaign or in the electoral process for this type of activity, and we will not permit or condone it."

Bernie Bloch knew better.

For many years, before Nino Osti, Dino Borelli was the Polo Lounge host at cocktail-hour.

Osti came to the hotel in 1968 after working eight years at La Rue, one of the few fine restaurants in Los Angeles at that time. The other choices were Chasen's, Romanoff's, Scandia, or a flight to San Francisco.

Ben Silberstein ate at La Rue and was impressed with Osti, who trained in Swiss hotels. "I need someone like you at the Beverly Hills," Silberstein said more than once.

Osti, who had met many of Los Angeles' more prominent people while at La Rue, thought he might open his own restaurant. While he was getting details worked out, he decided to take Silberstein up on his offer of employment, emphasizing it would be only a temporary arrangement. "I only came to help out for awhile. If it felt right, I might stay."

Silberstein had grabbed Osti's arms, "Look, I want you happy here," he had said. "You'll meet the most respected people in the world here. The Beverly Hills is something special."

One of the people Osti met was game-show producer Mark Goodson, who asked Nino if he was interested in appearing on *To Tell The Truth*. Nino didn't see why not. Sometime later, on a Wednesday at 7 p.m., Nino got a call from someone on the show's staff. Had Nino changed his mind, would he still go on the show? Again Nino agreed, thinking he would have a month, maybe more, to prepare. To his surprise, he was asked to be at the studio that Friday.

Osti appeared on a special segment of the show where instead of three people claiming to be the same person attempt to stump a celebrity panel, Osti would tell two different stories to a randomly selected member of the audience. The celebrities and the audience member got to question Osti before the girl, in this case, guessed which story was true. Osti, of course, knew the panel from their visits to the Polo Lounge. Soupy Sales kept looking down, trying not to give anything away.

In one story Osti claimed to own a fleet of gondolas in Venice. In the other, he told the truth. The panel asked questions about which were the best booths in the Polo Lounge, and Osti answered them so knowledgeably that he thought "Oh no, I'm giving myself away." The girl picked him as the gondola owner. After the show Osti's wife berated him. Didn't he feel sorry for that poor young girl? Why didn't he let her win? Osti's defense was he couldn't see she was a "poor young girl" because of the lights.

Osti never opened his restaurant. He stayed on at the hotel. While he was still lunch host, a local magazine named him one of The Ten Most Important People in Beverly Hills.

Other hotel stars were unquestionably the affable Sven with his Nordic-god looks, at the pool, and Peruvian-born Alex Olmeda, the 1959 Australian singles champion, on the tennis courts.

Hotels are notorious for high staff turnover. The Beverly Hills was the exception—except that is for those in the top management offices, many of whom did not enjoy the same longevity as the rest of the staff.

When Courtright left in 1958, Silberstein promoted Assistant Treasurer Stewart Hathaway to executive vice-president and managing director.

Silberstein liked Hathaway's style. Courtly, with gray hair, Hathaway dressed in impeccable suits and was a stickler for appearance. He would do the white-glove test for dust and lined up the desk clerks each day to inspect the shines on their shoes and the creases in their pants. One employee who worked at the hotel briefly, in 1957, remembered being stopped on his first day by Hathaway. "Where is your tie?" Hathaway wanted to know. "Can you afford a tie? If you can't, get an advance on your pay and buy a good one. This is the Beverly Hills, you know. This is not the Ambassador."

Hathaway fell out of favor when he was unable to bring back the Old Guard, the Main Line Philadelphians, the proper Bostonians, the Palm Beach and Greenwich, Connecticut, crowd to the hotel. Silberstein wanted them. He wanted the old rich, the Pasadenans, who continued to prefer the tiny Bel-Air.

This reason for Hathaway's decline was later denied by Burton Slatkin, who said that Hathaway was moved upstairs to a seat on the board of directors because "as happens to all of us, Stewart grew older." (Slatkin made that statement prior to the days of age discrimination suits.) For whatever the reason, Hathaway was stripped of power and was used primarily for public relations purposes. He was left with little to do besides count the $25,000 in cash he kept in a hotel safe deposit box—something he did every day.

His successor was Wallie Durden, who had been with the hotel for years. Durden was a social creature with a social wife, Jewell Curtis Cohn, a niece of the former Columbia Pictures dictator Harry Cohn.

Durden found that being manager didn't mean what it once had. He wasn't running the hotel; he was a glorified deskman.

The real power had slipped past him into the hands of an outsider, Martin Rubin, a moneyman lured by Silberstein from the United California Bank, to be financial vice-president.

It must have been a letdown for Durden, to be manager in name only, but as one observer noted, "He wasn't a qualified hotelman," and the Beverly Hills Hotel was no place for on-the-job manager training.

Overcoming any disappointment, Durden stayed on. His wife had money, and his title had prestige. There was also the fringe benefit of a house account, which meant free wining and dining of his friends. His socializing proved to be his downfall. In 1969, according to insiders, Silberstein noticed something disturbing.

Durden and Jewell were getting more publicity than the hotel. That wouldn't do. A manager shouldn't be more famous than what he was managing.

On top of which Silberstein was said not to have been terribly fond of Jewell. She always had a word of advice here, a suggestion there. She liked to run things from a banquette in the Polo Lounge. But worse, Silberstein didn't like her voice, which carried from from one end of the room to the other. Her voice did not belong at the Beverly Hills Hotel.

So one day, rather suddenly to anyone but an insider, Silberstein fired Durden.

"With barely more than a whistle," as one employee put it, "Durden was gone."

(Not entirely forgotten, however. After moving to the Fountainebleau in Miami Beach, Durden got in touch with his former secretary, still at the Beverly Hills. He had her forward him Beverly Hills computer printouts listing guests and their home addresses. He then sent these guests little notes about how nice it was to have known them in California and how he hoped that they would come to see him in Miami. The secretary was caught when she was about to send more lists and was fired.)

It was now Rubin's show, to the dismay of some of the employees.

They feared he would change the character of the hotel with parsimonious policies. He was, after all, known for reducing costs by crossing out overtime on their time cards. What if Rubin started cutting costs, pinching pennies when it came to guest services, turning the Beverly Hills into a Holiday Inn with parking attendants?

Rubin, a smiling Mr. Steel, gave the staff other reasons to fear him.

An employee on an errand to Rubin's office, which was off the downstairs arcade, was asked to wait while Rubin made a long-distance call to a woman who had worked for the hotel for thirteen years. She was vacationing.

"Hello," the Beverly Hills end of the conversation went. "This is Mr. Rubin at the hotel. . . .I'm fine. . . . Yes, about your vacation. You needn't bother coming back. You're fired. . . . Yes, that will be all taken care of. Goodbye."

The employee couldn't believe what he had heard. Rubin only chuckled.

"I hated to ruin her vacation, but that's when I usually tell people they're fired, when they are on vacation."

This man is a gem, the employee thought to himself.

Rubin was not to last, either. There were various versions of what caused his downfall.

The official one was simply that he wasn't doing his job. Rubin "was terminated after seven years because of a growing difference in policy matters between Silberstein and him."

But there were many observers who dismissed the official version. They saw it as Muriel wanting her husband in charge, and Silberstein liking to give his daughter what she wanted.

One day Silberstein picked a fight with Rubin, a shouting match that lasted all day, and threw him out before he could collect his pencils.

Rubin went to San Diego to a hotel owned by one of Richard Nixon's monied buddies. When the buddy ran into trouble with the IRS, Rubin returned to Los Angeles and attempted to emulate Hernando Courtright by competing with the Beverly Hills, at the Carriage House in Westwood. Hotel analysts felt that with a few more millions and a few more years, the Carriage House would have been a success. But Rubin and his backers did not have the luxury of that time or money and sold out. The Carriage House became the Sunset Hyatt House.

Slatkin took over the management of the hotel, which once again went to show that blood is thicker than the ink on a business-school diploma.

chapter eight

Ninteen-seventy-nine brought bad news to Ben Silberstein. He was diagnosed as having terminal pancreatic cancer. It was time for him to put his house in order.

He flew to Georgia where he spent two weeks with Rosalind, the ex-wife who had run him out of California, with whom there had been so much hatred.

He saw to it that Muriel *and* Burton would share her percentage of the hotel. Silberstein wanted them to stay together, if for no other reason than he saw his Slatkin grandsons, Tom and Edward, someday taking over the management and continuing his dynasty. It was a legacy, along with all the charitable contributions he had made over the years, for Ben Silberstein to leave.

Silberstein had always liked Burt Slatkin. He was the Good-Son-in-Law, the "son Ben Silberstein never had," as Dominick Dunne put it in *Vanity Fair.* Slatkin's family had a jewelry store in Detroit. After he and Muriel were married, in the early sixties, he went to work for his father-in-law.

Some hotel employees felt sorry for Slatkin. "Silberstein treated him like a piece of dirt," one remembered, "as did Muriel. He put his thumb on his son-law and never let up."

Slatkin used to follow Silberstein "around like a puppy dog, with Mr. S. throwing orders at him."

This treatment may not have been a true reflection of Silberstein's feelings for his son-in-law. As Bonnie Silberstein once said to Nino Osti, "My husband can be rude, but he regrets it later."

(To illustrate Silberstein's abrasiveness, Dominick Dunne told of the time that RCA's General David Sarnoff ran into Silberstein in the coffee shop at breakfast. "I spend so much time here, you should give me a discount," Sarnoff said.

"I'm thinking of charging more for people who stay here too long," Silberstein growled back.)

Silberstein had promoted Slatkin to president and chief operating officer of the hotel in 1973, but continued to run the show himself. Now with his death approaching, he wanted the hotel left to Slatkin's management.

Silberstein had reason to worry about the Slatkin marriage. There had been indications it was not in the soundest shape, the least of which was the repartee some mornings between Muriel and the bellman everyone hated, Dirty Mouth Dean.

"Did you get any last night, Muriel?" the bellman would ask.

No, Burton's not giving it to me anymore, she answered, using different terminology.

Then there was the stockbroker who handled Silberstein's portfolio. The man confided to friends he was having trouble with Muriel. As one of the friends put it, "Muriel had a sweet tooth for him. So she had his hotel room bugged to find out who he was going out with. Then she let the cat out of the bag. She must have shown she knew too much about what he was doing. Anyway, the guy went to Silberstein and said if he wanted him to continue making money for him, handling his portfolio, Silberstein would have to rein in his daughter."

Attaching Slatkin to the hotel would keep the marriage together. The hotel was Muriel's life. It gave her social credentials and clout—although it never got her into the Amazing Blue Ribbon, *the* women's group. Still being proprietor of the Beverly Hills Hotel, as her pink and green business cards proclaimed, meant frequent mentions in the columns, holding court at her double cabana at the pool, throwing big parties for big names, being good friends with Grace Robbins (Mrs. Harold *The Carpetbaggers* Robbins), Christina Onassis, *Los Angeles Times* society maven Jody Jacobs, Mrs. Sammy Cahn. (Songwriter Cahn married the much younger and somewhat taller former model Tita Curtis, August 2, 1970, at the hotel. The joke at the wedding was "Let's hope the marriage lasts as long as the reception." It did since she was still Mrs. Cahn at the time of his death in 1993.) There were many Muriel loyalists, but even her friends had to admit that she said whatever she was thinking, sometimes with little regard for tact.

If Burton Slatkin was the Good Son-in-Law, it fell to Seema's husband to be the bad one. Seema met her husband-to-be in the early sixties in Detroit. When she took him to meet her father, the young man announced that he intended to keep Seema "in the manner to which she was accustomed." Silberstein took an immediate dislike to him. The boyfriend boasted of having been graduated from the exclusive Cranbrook School and having gotten a degree from Silberstein's alma mater, the Detroit College of Law, but he was little more than a strip joint operator in the eyes of Seema's father.

Silberstein was to refer to Seema's husband—they were married in 1962, only nine months after they met—as "the bum" for as long as he lived. The rest of the world would come to refer to him in many other terms, for Seema Silberstein had married Ivan Boesky.

Boesky came from a upper middle-class Jewish family. His father was one of five Russian immigrant brothers. An uncle owned delicatessans known for the thinness of the corned beef slices. Boesky's father, William, owned a chain of bars, all named the Brass Rail.

According to other family members, from the time Ivan was ten, he ran the family. As the only son, he was the prince, catered to and excused. "He grew up to be a little Napoleon, totally convinced he was better than everybody else.... He was never taught the rules. Never."

In 1949, twelve-year-old Ivan entered the prestigious private school, Cranbrook. He excelled on the wrestling team, fueled by intensity and dedication. At one point, he was so determined to keep his weight down, his coach had to order him to stop dieting.

After his sophomore year, he left Cranbrook for Mumford, the public high school that was immortalized in Eddie Murphy's *Beverly Hills Cop*. An unidentified Boesky relative has said that Ivan was "expelled for cheating. I don't know exactly what he did, but he definitely was expelled." During Boesky's Wall Street heyday, he would claim he had been graduated from Cranbrook.

After high school, Boesky was in and out of several colleges and spent a year in Iran with his Cranbrook friend, Houshang Wekili. (Another self-aggrandizing claim Boesky made was that he worked for the CIA during this period, although no one has been able to verify it.)

In 1960, after returning to the States, Ivan joined the family business at his father's insistence. Ivan, who was going to law school, felt working in a bar was beneath him, but had little choice. There was only one Brass Rail by this time, in a downtown neighborhood, Great Circus Park, that was in transistion. The young middle class was abandoning it for the suburbs, and the Brass Rail, which had become a popular family spot, hemorraghed customers.

Bill Boesky, to lure in a new clientele, conventioneers, opened a special basement room for strippers. One of Ivan's duties was to hire the dancers. It was he who found Loddie the Body.

Little wonder Ben Silberstein looked upon this seeker of his daughter's hand with a jaundiced eye.

Boesky put the bar into bankruptcy in 1966 after his father died. He was working as an accountant when a Cranbrook wrestling-friend told him about the world of arbitrage. Boesky moved to New York City to try his hand at it.

When looked at from a certain perspective, arbitrage is little more than a Las Vegas crap shoot. The arbitrageur—or, arb—buys large blocks of stock in a company caught up in a takeover bid. The arb is betting the eventual takeover price will be higher than what he paid for the stock. If he bets correctly, he's a winner and the payoff can be considerable. If he's wrong, if the takeover falls through or the stock purchase price is lower than the arb paid, it's snake eyes.

Boesky got a job with L. F. Rothschild & Company, then bounced around to other firms. He was fired from Kalb Voorhis when he lost $20,000 on a single deal.

Although he had promised Silberstein to provide Seema with those creature comforts to which she was accustomed, it fell to daddy to help them out when Boesky was between jobs. Reportedly, it was Silberstein who set them up in their Park Avenue apartment and provided Seema with the wherewithal to hang Renoirs on the wall.

In 1972 the firm of Edwards and Hanley asked Boesky to set up an arbitrage department. He did. It was then that he had his first run-in with federal regulators. The New York Stock Exchange censured him for selling short more stock than he had been able to borrow for delivery, and the

Securities and Exchange Commission slapped him with a $10,000 fine.

Boesky was without a job in 1975 when Edwards and Hanley went bankrupt. However, he wasn't without resources. Boesky opened Ivan F. Boesky and Company with a bankroll of $700,000. The money was said to have come from his mother, though Barbara Walters later reported it was Seema's "money that launched him into business," and James B. Stewart, in *Den of Thieves*, wrote that it came from Seema's mother and her husband, a Detroit doctor.

Whatever the case, Boesky had found his milieu. "I'm lucky I found the field," he told Terry Bivens of the *Philadelphia Inquirer* in 1984.

The fact that Boesky began making big money and could afford to have a limousine take him to and from work did not impress his father-in-law. According to Muriel, "My father was always disappointed in my sister's choice of husband."

Silberstein was once overheard talking to a close friend of his, who was also friendly with the Boeskys. "So what do you think of your son-in-law now?" the friend asked.

Silberstein shrugged disdainfully, "Yeah, he makes a lot of money. What good is it?"

Whether it was dislike, disdain, or distrust, Seema's share in the hotel was in her name only.

Silberstein's condition worsened, and he was hospitalized at the UCLA Medical Center. Muriel visited him daily and often complained that her sister wasn't there enough. Although Muriel professed to love her sister, there was obvious ambivalence between them. Muriel ascribed the tension to Seema's childhood jealousy. "My sister was heavy and not as popular as me." (That Muriel was less than fond of her sister was evidenced when this book was first written. The Slatkins were allowed to read the manuscript for accuracy. Muriel penciled parentheses around the one paragraph that mentioned her sister's married name, but did not correct the misspelling of "Boesky.")

When Dominick Dunne was doing his piece on the sisters for *Vanity Fair*, someone likened them to Goneril and Regan in *King Lear* "...with the father manipulating it all." People who knew the family felt that Ben had always favored Muriel—he did buy the hotel for her. Muriel argued that wasn't the case. "... father approved of my husband and despised Ivan. I was always the peacemaker in the family, and I would say to my father, 'Don't make Seema miserable because you don't approve of her husband.'"

Ben Silberstein's manipulation, or at least his direct meddling, was to end on December 19, 1979, with his death at the age of seventy-seven. His obituary was headlined "Host To Stars Dies."

A *Los Angeles Times* story, citing California court records, had Muriel and Burton Slatkin receiving 41.5 percent of the stock, Seema 38.5 percent, and Silberstein's sister, Gertrude Marks, 20 percent. Most other sources put the division at an equal split of 48 percent for the Slaktins and Seema, and 4 percent for Gertrude Marks.

Bonnie Silberstein, in accordance with the prenuptial agreement, received no shares in the hotel, althouth she came away with apartments in Palm Beach and on New York's Sutton Place and visiting privileges at the hotel. (Bonnie was to outlive her husband by only a few years.)

In all likelihood, the story of the Beverly Hills Hotel would read much differently had Gertrude Marks not died less than a year after her brother, in May 1980. She left her shares in the hotel to her son, Royal, a concert pianist turned New York art dealer, and daughter, Sybil Barere.

The Slatkins had approached Gertrude before her death offering to buy her swing shares. She named a price that the

Slatkins felt was far too high. "Burt's tight," someone told Dominick Dunne. "He lost the fucking hotel because he's tight. When you're in a takeover, you don't quibble over money. If the old lady wanted a hundred bucks, you give her three, and if she wanted a million bucks, you give her three million."

After Gertrude's death, Boesky went to Royal Marks and gave him what he asked. It was a palace coup. By January 1981, Ivan and Seema had 52 percent of the shares and control of the board of directors of the hotel's parent corporation. Muriel was furious but powerless. If there had been friction before between the Silberstein girls, there was now enmity. The two stopped speaking.

The question was what would the Boeskys do? And the answer was—nothing. (Although Boesky did demand that Bonnie be put it better rooms on her visits.) The hotel continued to be run as it had been before Silberstein's death. "Boesky was lucky," it was pointed out. "The hotel could pretty much run itself."

Of course, Ivan Boesky was busy in the early part of the eighties. At about the same time he was getting control of the Hills, he liquidated Ivan F. Boesky and Company and set about raising funds for his new firm, the Ivan F. Boesky Corporation.

He suffered one disaster in 1982 when Gulf Oil made a friendly offer for Cities Service. Boesky jumped in and bought a hugh block of stock, only to have Gulf back off. Occidental then came in and bought Cities Service for $8 a share less than Gulf had offered. It's estimated that Boesky was clobbered with an $11 million loss. Seema was heard to say, "As far as I'm concerned this is never going to happen again. Never again." It was assumed she meant Ivan would not be allowed to risk the family money like that again. By mid-1983 he had aligned himself with Michael Milken of

Drexel Burnham Lambert in the dizzying labyrinth of dirty deals that lead to prison cells for both of them.

Whenever Boesky met with Milken in Beverly Hills, he stayed in his favorite suite, 135-36. It was conveniently located on the ground floor with a nearby door leading outside. The staff saw women who were not Seema coming in and exiting through that door. "They were sneaking in and out. The Slatkins would have loved it if they had known." But the staff had always adhered to a strict code of discretion, and this was to be no exception.

Besides being Boesky's West Coast base of operation, the hotel figured into his association with Drexel in another respect. In the late seventies, Milken started a yearly conference to promote his high-yield bonds. By 1983, the conference, which earned the nickname "The Predator's Ball," for all the corporate raiders that attended, was going strong. The conference was not held at the Beverly Hills Hotel, but one of the big events was the Thursday evening cocktail party thrown by Donald Engel of Drexel. Engel had a reputation of pandering to his client's baser instincts. "Corporate America likes women," he once said. "Find a hooker and you'll find a client."

The no-wives party was held in Bungalow 8, and by 1986 the guest list had climbed into the hundreds. In attendance that year was Marvin Davis, the former oil wildcatter, who had already branched out into many other fields.

Burton Slatkin continued to manage the hotel, although his marriage to Muriel was disintegrating. He moved out of the Regency mansion, and she found herself a younger boyfriend, a Chilean named Ricardo Pascal.

During this period, Boesky came and went. He was treated like any other guest, except for certain perks. For instance, he would tell Alex Olmeda that he planned to use the tennis court, but wasn't sure when. He would instruct the pro to keep both courts clear all day. Of course, this meant Olmeda lost income from the lessons he might have been giving. Boesky never offered to compensate him. One of the other pros was Sam, a young Thai from a well-to-do family, who had played on his country's Davis Cup team. During their lessons, Boesky would cruelly tease Sam for his accented English. The Thai was not surprised by Boesky's later troubles. The arb cheated on line calls.

Then everything changed. In July 1985, Boesky called an extraordinary meeting of the entire staff. Elisa Dadian, an assistant manager since 1980, described it as "historic." Never before was there a meeting held for everyone, from potscrubbers to manager. Someone has to stay on duty to run the hotel. But not this time. Boesky had all 415 employees assemble in the Crystal Room where he announced that from that moment on Burton Slatkin would no longer be president and chief executive officer of the hotel. Adalberto M. Stratta, who had been president of Princess Hotels International, was replacing him. Although Slatkin was named chairman of the board, everyone in the room knew he'd been rendered impotent. Everyone knew his executive power was gone. Muriel quickly left the room.

What followed must have been a worst-feared nightmare for her. She was thrown out of her office and cabana, although she could rent the latter by the day if it wasn't already booked. She lost her prized table in the Polo Lounge and her ten percent discount at the drugstore. And the story went around town—gossip spreads through Beverly Hills like a cold in a nursery school—that when she tried to charge dinner at a local restaurant, she discovered her hotel credit cards had been cancelled.

A friend reported that "she was so embarrassed she didn't dare walk through the lobby." Further, she was so depressed that she took to her bed for six weeks, seeing only Pascal and a few close friends. The rumor mill had her hospitalized.

It didn't take Muriel long to bounce back. She and Slatkin hired Washington lawyer Edward Bennett Williams to represent them. For one thing, they wanted to sell the hotel. The Boeskys didn't.

It was all-out war. In May of 1985, the Slatkins filed a suit in Los Angeles federal court seeking the sale of the hotel *plus* $100 million in damages. They accused Boesky of using hotel money for stock speculation—specifically in his Cities Service debacle of 1982. They claimed the hotel corporation took a $7.6 million hit after Boesky used $13 million in hotel money in his arbitrage maneuvers.

Seema came back with a thirty-six page declaration accusing her sister and husband, Burton, of "offensive and abusive treatment" and using "extortion" in trying to get the hotel placed on the market. She stated further that any losses that may have been incurred were made up for by $9.1 million in profits the hotel enjoyed from a Minneapolis television station Boesky bought for the hotel corporation's portfolio.

The Boeskys won the first round of what promised to be a long court fight when the Slatkin suit was dismissed in September 1985 on procedural grounds. According to the laws of Delaware, where the hotel's parent company was incorporated, Muriel should have sought satisfaction first from the hotel's board.

Whatever Muriel was planning as her next move didn't matter after October 14, 1986. That was the day the SEC announced that Boesky had agreed to settle charges that he had traded on illegal inside information. The man who had written a book on how to be the number-one arbitrageur in the world had left out the chapter on how he cheated. Boesky, who didn't tell Seema about his crimes until just before the SEC's shocking announcement, was to pay $50 million in fines and return $50 million in illegal profits and was never to engage in the securities business in the United States again.

Muriel was in gloater's heaven. It was "sweet revenge," she told an *L.A. Times* reporter right before calling her brother-in-law "greedy" and "pompous." She expressed no concern for her sister, whose life had been shot to pieces. Seema, unlike her sister, had been a private person, never looking for ink in the society columns. She suddenly found herself sucked into one of the worst maelstroms in American financial history. Her husband would be reviled not only for his crimes but for cooperating with investigators and turning on former colleagues. It was at the Beverly Hills Hotel that Boesky wore a wire in an attempt to get Michael Milken to incriminate himself. As James B. Stewart wrote, "Nothing Milken said would be a 'smoking gun' at any future trial, but the tape would be useful probative evidence. Milken never denied the existence of their scheme; he'd never denied Boesky owed him money…The whole discussion made little sense unless Boesky's version of the conspiracy were, in fact, true."

Beyond the humiliation of Boesky's crimes, Seema had to face his infidelities. In a 1992 televised interview, she told Barbara Walters that she had been ready to stand by her husband. "I was there for better or worse and forever. However, I had said, before we were married that if I was ever embarrassed or disgraced by his cheating, I would leave. [Her father had told her that all men had affairs. They didn't matter as long as they weren't serious.] And ten days after the announcement, I found out that Ivan had a woman, and she was actually living in the building we had an apartment in. And that was it for me. The day I found out, we separated."

In time Seema would seek a divorce, and Boesky would respond by asking for $20,000 a week alimony. Ivan argued that he "should not be forced to incur futher debt while

Seema redecorates the marital estate ..."—a 17-room house set on 200 acres in Mount Kisco, New York, which she says was bought with her own money.

But that was to come. In 1986, the sisters finally found something they could agree on. It was time to sell the hotel. Brooks Harvey, the real estate arm of Morgan Stanley & Company, would handle the November auction of the hotel, with minimum bids of $100 million. There were reportedly eight bidders including Merv Griffin, Marvin Davis, Donald Trump, and the sultan of Brunei.

Seema held up the final sale for a brief period because she "was afraid money from the sale could be entangled in litigation stemming from the widening government investigation of her husband's insider stock trading activities," a source told the *L. A. Times*.

Her fears were allayed: on December 8, 1986, the new owner of the Beverly Hills Hotel was announced. And the winner was ...

chapter nine

...Marvin Davis.

Like Ivan Boesky, Marvin Davis is a symbol of the excesses of the eighties, a decade of Ronald Reagan's voodoo economics run amok. In 1986, Davis was still riding high with a reputation as a daring businessman who went after what he wanted and made gobs of money in the process.

He had all the trappings. The 727 jet parked on the tarmac. The $20 million Beverly Hills home purchased from singer Kenny Rogers in 1984, which made it one of the most expensive private residences in the United States.

But much of what he and Boesky and their ilk was was what they were hyped. A few flattering stories and suddenly they were the shrewdest, the canniest, the most intuitive spotters of good deals and companies. The public was led to believe that these Midases were hands-on healers of ailing companies. But as Wayne and Garth would say, "NOT."

Aetna Life and Casualty Company president John H. Filer went into a meeting with the 6'6", 300-pound Davis in 1981 having read some of the clips. Davis was described as the "nation's leading oilman." He was supposed to have had $600 million in investments with 400 wells working around the clock to pump up more wealth. He had celebrity investors flocking to him for a piece of his action, *Star Wars* wizard George Lucas, former Secretary of State Henry Kissinger, former President Gerald Ford, and comedienne Lucille Ball, among others.

Filer, whose company had $39.8 billion in assets, was eager to become involved with Davis. When they walked out of the Hartford, Connecticut restaurant, Davis had a $50 million Aetna commitment. (This led one of the insurance company employees to joke, "Maybe [they should] send down the napkin they figured this out on.")

Within a year, Filer had okayed another $168 million. But Davis was starting to cast his net out beyond the oil fields. He wanted to become another Kolberg, Kravis, Roberts, building an empire of many different companies. As it turned out, Davis wasn't to get many of the big ones he went after. He lost out on CBS, Resorts International, and Northwest Airlines. (Northwest had been a desirable target because its frugal management had run the airline with little debt. The company was so cost-conscious that one president had the doors removed from the men's room stalls so that executives wouldn't waste time reading in them.) Wall Street came to look upon Davis, as *Business Week* put it in 1989, "as just another in-and-out trader aiming to make enough noise to move the stock up a few points."

The sale of stock used to be an instrument to raise capital. In the last twenty years it became a weapon used by outsiders in raids against other companies. Often when these modern pirates were successful, they had to gut the companies to pay off the massive debt racked up in the purchase.

Even when Davis was able to buy a company, he let others run it. An exception was 20th Century-Fox, which he bought in 1981 for $725 million with Marc Rich.

(Rich, who runs a global commodities business, has been listed in the Forbes directory of the four hundred richest Americans. He's also listed on the federal government's wanted list. In 1983 he was accused of income tax evasion for not reporting profits made from rigging the price of crude oil during the 1979 energy crisis. Rich paid $172 million in taxes and penalties, then left the country, fearing a trial that could have brought him up to three hundred years in prison.)

It was bad enough that Davis saddled the studio with $650 million in debt to pay back the $550 million he and Rich had borrowed for the purchase, the oilman suddenly fancied himself an Irving Thalberg. Davis was making decisions on properties and stars. Remember *Rhinestone*, a 1984 Dolly Parton-Sylvester Stallone vehicle that one reviewer called "profoundly unfunny"? *Unfaithfully Yours* with Dudley Moore? Don't want to? These bombs fell courtesy of Marvin Davis. And Davis lost the incredibly successful producing team of Richard Zanuck and David Brown, who had brought *Jaws* and many other hits to the screen, when he had their expense accounts audited.

In 1984, Davis persuaded Barry Diller to come over from Paramount Pictures. Diller, famous as much for his long romance with designer Diane von Furstenberg as for his phenomenal studio successes, had been unhappy at Paramount since *Martin* Davis—things were pretty confusing in Hollywood for awhile with the two Davises, separated by only one letter in their names—had taken over as chairman of the parent company, Gulf and Western, after the death of Charles Bludhorn.

There is a question about whether Diller was fired, as Martin Davis implied in an in-company memo, or whether he jumped ship. In either case, he arrived at Fox with 25 percent ownership of the company given to him by Marvin Davis as part of the employment package.

At the time Liz Smith wrote, "Fox has nowhere to go but up, and everybody knows it. And Diller's rewards should be fantastic if he can overhaul Fox's creative and money-making process. Yesterday the *Wall Street Journal* minced no words in describing Fox owner Marvin Davis as a man who likes to meddle and control. So the question is—will Big Marvin leave his new studio chief alone, allowing Diller to make it work?"

There was no time for the question to be answered. Diller came to Fox, with his 25 percent, and, according to him, discovered something Davis had neglected to mention. Not only was the studio staggering under the debt, but by 1985, under Davis's stewardship, it was looking at $200 million in losses. Diller began making noises about suing but didn't follow through when Davis sold the company to media tycoon Rupert Murdoch for $325 million in cash along with some property that included the 5,300-acre Pebble Beach golf complex.

If the the people on staff at the Beverly Hills Hotel had read the *Wall Street Journal*'s description of Davis as being meddlesome and controlling, they might not have been so happy when he emerged the winner. There had been fears that a big corporation—or foreigners—would not understand what they had bought and would treat the Beverly Hills as another entry in the ledger book. The wrong ownership might not recognize the hotel for the grand old lady she was. As Ernie Brown pointed out, "It survived for eighty years and reached a high point, with a worldwide reputation. If you asked anyone in Europe at the fine hotels where they stayed when they were in Los Angeles, the answer always was the Beverly Hills Hotel. It was a country club for the right people."

Davis made a big point of his fondness for the hotel and was a longtime guest. He and wife Barbara had honeymooned there, and his family occupied Bungalow 1 (paying the full daily rate and running up an annual bill of $300,000) for four-and-a-half years before he bought the Kenny Rogers house.

"Everyone was totally relieved when [Marvin Davis] bought [the hotel]," actor Christopher Plummer, a guest of many years, said, "instead of a giant chain of hotels that wouldn't have paid any attention to any of the hotel's traditions."

The new regime didn't start auspiciously. Davis called in a team of high-priced consultants to examine the operation and find ways to improve it. As assistant manager Elisa Dadian has since observed, "That was the fashion in the eighties, to bring in consultants.... They had lots of big titles, but they didn't know what they were doing. They charged $500,000 for the black book they prepared for Davis. As Carl Icahn said, this kind of thing means nothing. Davis did not put his faith in the 'little people' like us." These little people were the ones who knew the clientele and had been running the hotel so successfully for so many years.

Alberto Stratta left. He saw the handwriting on the front office wall. Stratta was too good and too prominent in the business to conform to Marvin Davis' style and to report to Marvin Davis's people. According to Dadian, "Everyone was crying when Stratta left. Even the maids were in tears."

Davis should have been crying as well since Stratta, as Nino Osti put it, "got on beautifully with the guests." Stratta eventually returned to the east to teach hotel management.

Davis also fired several staff members and put the rest on probation. One insider remarked, "He got rid of a lot people before he discovered the hotel doesn't run itself."

Outsiders would not have gotten the impression that Davis was having any problems at the hotel. At the beginning of May, the *Los Angeles Times* ran a glowing story about how much fun Davis was having with the Hills. "I found it's a great pride and joy to own something like this." The hotel, he explained, had been "a mecca for every business I've ever been in."

He set himself up at the Polo Lounge table facing the entrance—the *Times* story included the very strange aside that "Some people say the reason the former owners of the Beverly Hills Hotel started fighting is that Muriel Slatkin wanted to call that spot hers"—and took to glad-handing. "People like to say hello to you, and I like to say hello to people. Unfortunately I'm in so many other ventures that my time is limited. But the few good hours I spend on breakfasts and lunches give me a pretty good feel for what's right and wrong about the hotel."

There were still a lot of interesting people to say hello to at the Hills. Staying there at Academy Awards time that year were Sigourney Weaver, Ismail Merchant and James Ivory, the *A Room with a View* team, and Dianne Wiest. And of course, there were the regulars like Sir Richard Attenborough, Diana Ross, Liza Minnelli (her stepmother, Lee Minnelli says that "Liza always stays there with her entourage"), and Elizabeth Taylor.

Davis had announced he would spend $40 million dollars refurbishing. When asked what he thought of what Caroline Hunt Schoellkopf—who was now the richest of the Hunt family, after the brothers' fiasco in the silver market—had done with the Bel-Air, Davis answered, "I think [she] did a wonderful job of refurbishing an old hotel. And we hope that ours will be done as well."

People at the Hills were in agreement that the hotel needed work, but they were increasingly alarmed by Davis's approach. He talked about how he liked the food there, but changed chefs. He was proud of bringing the fat pork sausages from Pebble Beach and putting them on the breakfast menu—no wonder this man was three hundred pounds—but he wanted to get rid of the guacamole. *THE GUACAMOLE!*

People began to complain about the food. The courtly Joseph Cotten was not one to complain, but when he made a rare trip to the hotel for lunch—he had suffered a stroke in 1981—he lamented the fact that chicken crepes, after forty years, were no longer on the menu. At one time, Cotten and his wife, actress Patricia Medina, were frequent diners at the hotel. "They always wanted the first table on the Patio," according to Nino Osti.

The staff was beginning look upon Davis as someone who was a nice guest, but you didn't want him as an owner.

"The staff didn't know how to say 'no' to anyone," one insider said in explanation of the story he told about the wedding of Davis's daughter.

According to the insider, "Mrs. Davis called Rita Corwin of catering and said she wanted Rita to handle the daughter's wedding in Denver, all the food, flowers, music, the whole thing. So Rita did. She used the people she had dealt with for years at the Hills. She brought them in and flew them to Denver.

"After the party, Mrs. Davis called Rita. 'Everything was fine, but we're going to pay everyone only 50 percent of their bills. Tell them there's no use suing. My husband has ten lawyers on the payroll with nothing better to do than handle this.'"

On another occasion, Barbara Davis told a staff member to get a birthday cake from Hansen's, a very expensive bakery that will draw a likeness of the guest of honor in the icing. The staff member asked if Mrs. Davis wanted anything done to the cake.

"No, serve it exactly as it is." Which it was. When the cake was brought out, Mrs. Davis was furious. The candles, where were the candles? She tried to have the staffer fired for following her orders.

Sven from the pool quit when Davis announced that employees could no longer eat in the coffee shop.

Elisa Dadian had no problem when Davis put his son Gregg on her shift at the front desk as a trainee. Davis wanted Gregg to run the hotel eventually. She said Gregg was very conscientious. His hours were from 8:00 a.m. to 4:00 p.m. "He came exactly at eight and never left before four. I used him as an example to other employees."

She liked his unassuming attitude. He didn't come in throwing his father's weight around. "He would come to me and ask, 'Elisa, may I make a telephone call?' and I would say, 'Gregg, you own the place. Go ahead.'"

With Gregg at the front desk and Marvin turning the hotel into his "playground," as one of his friends put it, no one would have believed that Davis was already looking for a buyer. Within in a few months of acquiring the hotel, he was seeking to sell it.

The announcement came on Tuesday, October 6. The statement said little beyond that the hotel had been sold to Sajahtera Incorporated by the Miller-Klutznick-Davis-Gray Company. Lee Solters, one of Hollywood's top public relations men, said Davis had no comment. "He won't speak to anyone."

Sources told the *Los Angeles Times* that the sale had pretty much been a done deal in August.

Sajahtera belonged to the Sultan of Brunei, purportedly the richest man in the world. Davis received $185 million, a pretty good return considering the price he'd paid only ten months earlier was $136 million. However, the *Times* sources claimed revisions in the federal tax laws would keep Davis from realizing much of a profit, despite what it looked like. "It was a wash."

There are many staffers at the Hills who hope so. They view Davis's tenure there as "a total disaster." And because so many employees, past and present, saw the Hills as more than a paycheck, they resented what Davis did. "A lot of people at the Hills are hoping that justice will prevail," one said, "and Davis will be the next eighties high-flyer who crashes."

They, undoubtedly, followed Davis's travails with pleasure. Aetna had taken Davis to court, charging him with presenting optimistic projections, misrepresenting oil-well output, and hiding cost overruns. An audit found Davis's success ratios and returns to be below industry averages. You are what you're hyped, and by 1989 stories about Davis were headlined "The Marvin Davis Mystique: Less than meets the eye? His dealmaking has been more miss than hit ..."

Aetna wasn't the only one suing. There were several others. In 1988 a suit was brought by a former associate of Davis's, John A. Masek, who charged Davis with ordering many more pipe inspections than necessary. The inspection companies would give Davis a volume discount, the complaint claimed, that wasn't reported to stockholders. Davis would pocket the difference between the full price and the discounted price.

What mattered most to those at the Beverly Hills was the King was dead. It was now long live the Sultan.

chapter ten

The richest man in the world. The phrase is welded to the Sultan of Brunei's name. *The Sultan of Brunei, the richest man in the world.* More precisely, he is Duli Yang Maha Mulia Paduka Seri Baginda Sultan and Yang Di-Pertuan Negeri Brunei Awang Muda Hassanal Bolkiah Mu'issaddin Waddaulah Ibni Duli Yang Teramat Mulia Paduka Seri Begawan Sultan Awang Muda Omar Ali Aifuddin Saifuddin Sa'adul Khairi Waddin, the richest man in the world.

Sir Hassanal Bolkiah, to those close to him, has become famous around the world for his estimated income of $3 billion a year, but even most *Jeopardy* contestants would be hard pressed to find Brunei on the map. The country sounds vaguely Persian Gulf, maybe one of those emirates where American jets refueled during Operation Desert Storm.

It is, in fact, a tiny Muslim country of 2,226 square miles, about the size of Delaware, on the north coast of Borneo, along the South China Sea.

At one time, before the sixteenth century, Brunei had been a regional power. The kingdom included all of Borneo and most of the nearby Philippines. It is believed that Islam was introduced to the nation in the fifteenth century. Legend has it that the then-king was infatuated with a

Muslim princess from an island in what is now Malaysia. To impress her, the king converted.

The sixteenth century brought the Spanish, Dutch, and Portuguese, who carved up much of Brunei among them. The Bruneians turned to piracy and were apparently quite proficient at it. One Dutch navigator described them as "robust, well-built, intelligent, and dedicated to robbery."

Brunei continued to lose territory over the decades. The British showed up in the nineteenth century. After an uprising, which an English soldier quelled, Brunei lost its territories of Sabah and Sarawak. At this point it seemed prudent for the Bruneians to throw in with the British Empire, an if-you-join-them-then-maybe-they-won't-beat-you attitude. In 1888 the two countries signed a treaty that made Brunei an official protectorate of the United Kingdom, which meant London would take care of the small jungle nation's defense and foreign relations.

All of this would make Brunei of little interest except to students of Southeast Asia looking for a graduate thesis topic if it had not been for what occurred in 1929. It was in that year that the giant British-Dutch firm, Royal Dutch Shell discovered oil—lots of oil.

By 1980, Shell, in partnership with Brunei, was pumping 240,000 barrels a day. Adding even more to the sultanate's coffers, natural gas was found in 1965. Fifteen years later, five million metric tons of liquefied natural gas was being sent annually to Japan from a plant that was the largest in the world when it was built in 1972.

Today the country's per capita income—more than $20,000 a year—is among the highest in the world.

These vast riches made some of Brunei's neighbors, Indonesia in particular, jealous and covetous. Brunei was quite happy to be under Britain's protective umbrella. In 1959 the present sultan's father, Sir Oman, felt secure enough to allow the country its first constitution. The flirtation with democracy lasted until 1962, when the opposition party, which was calling for abolition of the monarchy and annexation by Indonesia, won a big victory. Suspecting Indonesia's meddling influence behind the dissent, Sir Oman suspended the constitution. The monarchy was saved by the timely intervention of a troop of Gurkha soldiers— fierce Nepalese warriors you wouldn't want to meet in a well-lit alley much less a dark one—flown in from Singapore.

This episode reinforced Brunei's desire to continue its arrangement with Great Britain. Whitehall, on the other hand, was increasingly uneasy with the lingering vestiges of colonialism. In 1967, when it became clear that London was going to insist on independence for Brunei, Sir Oman abdicated and yanked his twenty-one-year-old son, Sir Hassanal Bolkiah, out of Sandhurst, the British military academy, weeks before graduation.

Sir Oman figured that Britain would not walk away from an oil-rich country with a kid at the reins of power. His ploy paid off and Brunei enjoyed a few more years of British protection. For his part, Sir Hassanal Bolkiah had been reluctant to leave Sandhurst, but he obeyed his father's wishes and has been sultan ever since.

By most accounts—although there's no way of telling how many are the result of skillful public relations—the sultan is well thought of by his countrymen, and why not? Brunei is a country with no debt, no personal income tax, and most mortgages and car loans are interest free. Where interest is charged, the highest rate is 0.5 percent. (There are 55,000 cars in this country that, as late as the 1980s, only had 200 miles of paved road; that works out to one car for every two feet.) Citizens get subsidized, low-cost electricity, fuel, and basic foods.

If Brunei's five-hundred-bed hospital is unequipped to deal with a medical problem, the patient—and family—is flown to a foreign hospital with all expenses paid.

There is free schooling through the secondary level. Since Brunei has no university, thousands of qualified students are sent abroad to study, again with all expenses paid. An ulterior motive for the foreign study programs, is the sultan's concern that 46 percent of the country's work force (about 85,000) is in public service. Being a bureaucrat has been the most favored job in Brunei—probably because of the many additional perks, such as free trips to England. It is hoped that those going to schools overseas will come back with skills and aspirations for something other than pushing paper.

The sultan can afford all this largesse because of the vast sums the country makes from oil and natural gas. The wealth creates another reality, a sort of a parallel dimension that is hard for people living from paycheck to paycheck to comprehend.

For instance, with the approach of independence in 1984, the sultan had the world's largest palace built, with two thousand workers racing to complete it in time for the celebration.

The palace, set on 300 acres, has 1,778 rooms (about 400 more than the Vatican), more than 200 bathrooms (many with taps plated with 22-karat gold), 44 staircases, 18 elevators, 16 acres of Italian marble, a banquet hall that accommodates 4,000, a 100-car garage, 1,000 telephones, a throne room lined with solid gold tiles, an air-conditioned stable for 230 polo ponies, and a regulation-size polo field. (The sultan is an avid polo player who has been described as "very aggressive...but not world-class." When he flies to matches in his 727, he has the seats at the back taken out to make room for the ponies.)

The more-or-less official figure given for the cost of the palace is $250 million. Suppliers, however, put it closer to $600 million. Those little extras like 22-karat gold tiled interior arches tend to run up the tab.

(The palace's interior decorator was quoted as saying that "the sultan strived not to make it ostentatious.")

When one of the sultan's houses in London was burglarized in 1989, the thieves made off with $16 million in jewelry, gold, and foreign currency—but they had to leave behind $65 million in cash and jewels because they couldn't carry it.

In 1990, for his nephew, Prince Bahar's ninth birthday, the sultan took over London's Claridge Hotel ballroom. He had it transformed into the sewer-headquarters of the Teenage Mutant Ninja Turtles, had four actors dressed as Donatello, Raphael, Michaelangelo, and Leonardo (the turtles, not the painters) roaming the party, and, of course, served the Ninja Turtle's favorite food, pizza—all for a cost of $950,000.

In 1990, when he was wooing the sixteen-year-old daughter of a polo-playing friend, Sir Hassanal Bolkiah gave the young woman a $5 million emerald, her own helicopter, and an Aston Martin convertible with an 18-carat gold ignition key.

It's little wonder that in 1986 the sultan's name popped up in head of Assistant Secretary of State for Inter-American Affairs Elliot Abrams when the Reagan administration was looking for a way to circumvent Congress' two-year ban on funds for the Nicaraguan contras. The sultan was still worrying about Indonesia and possible external threats and was happy to do a favor for the powerful United States. Ten million? Sure. But where should the sultan deposit the money?

Abrams took his problem to the ever-resourceful Oliver North. North happened to have a number for a Swiss bank account into which the funds could be placed. Congress would be none the wiser. It was never ascertained who made the mistake, but either North or his secretary, Fawn Hall, transposed two digits in the number, and the ten million went into the wrong account. As the Iran-Contra scandal was hitting the fan, the State Department got to wondering about the ten million it had never seen. The money was traced to the account of a Swiss businessman, who claimed not to have realized the money wasn't his. The sultan demanded and got the ten million back—with interest. Ollie North got national attention. Elliot Abrams got two years probation. And George Bush said he was never in the loop, even as his nose grew longer and longer.

One might wonder why the sultan was adamant about getting a mere ten million back. Besides being annoyed that he was dragged into the scandal—Brunei claimed it thought the money was going to help the poor in Central America— the sultan had the future to think about. For as all things in life and the world are finite, even Brunei's party will come to an end. Geologists forecast the oil will run out at the turn of the century.

The sultan is keeping rich deposits of silica in reserve, but they won't support the country in the style to which it has become accustomed. Hence, Brunei's heavy foreign investments. The sultan and his advisers are hoping to amass enough of a portfolio to be able to live off the interest alone.

That's is why the richest man in the world cast his eye toward still another palace, the pink one on Sunset Boulevard.

News of the purchase came as a punch to the midriff in Beverly Hills. For one thing, no one knew that it was for sale. It was thought that all the angst over who would get it had been resolved when Marvin Davis closed the deal. And now...sold...again...to that sultan guy.

"I just hope the sultan doesn't turn it into another Caesars Palace," Jane Nathanson, a neighbor, worried, echoing the sentiments of many Beverly Hills residents. The city had already suffered through oil money tastelessness when the son of an Arabian sheik painted the statuary on his Sunset Boulevard estate garish colors, choosing especially stand-out hues for the genitalia.

The purchase came as a surprise even to the sultan's minister counsellor and director of communications back in Brunei. "You'll have to ask the sultan," he told the *Los Angeles Times*. When the reporter asked how he might reach the sultan, Haji Ampuan Saptu said, "Oh, my goodness, no, that would not be possible."

Beverly Hills waited for the other shoe to drop. What was the sultan going to do with their Pink Palace? There were rumors that he was going to close it to the public and use it as a private residence, an idea, which, on closer examination, sounded absurd, considering his palace back in Brunei. Also, he had done no such thing to the Dorchester in London after he purchased it in 1985. In fact, care had been taken in the restoration to retain its character.

Kerman Beriker was brought in as chief executive officer and general manager of the sultan's new hotel acquisition. He was general manager at the Bel-Air for a couple of years in the mid-eighties when Caroline Hunt Schoellkopf owned it. Ask the public relations office at the Bel-Air about him, and you'll be told he was a "good manager." The talk around Beverly Hills is that he was booted out. According to one hotel insider, "he'd like to be taken as Swiss—he says he went to school in Switzerland—but actually he's a Turkish Jew."

Beriker was said to make $250,000 a year at the Beverly Hills Hotel and owned several cars that the hotel purchased for him.

He did not go out of his way to ingratiate himself with the staff or the regulars. Elisa Dadian, for one, didn't care for his style. Dadian, who spoke five languages and handled many of the foreign visitors, felt he was uncomfortable with her because she was a woman, younger than he, and more familiar with the hotel's operation.

That he lacked an appreciation of what set the Hills apart from other hotels was evident in the way he alienated some of the locals.

Leonard Stanley, who can point out which side of the arcade Francis Taylor's art gallery was on and becomes wistful when he remembers the hotel's great parties, masked balls with Loretta Young and Lana Turner, stopped going to the hotel after a run-in with Beriker. For years, Stanley, who had decorated the Coterie restaurant for the Slatkins, had his dog Harry wear a red bandana before it was fashionable. He brought Harry along when he went to the hotel coffee shop, which was on the lower level and could be reached without going through the lobby. No one objected, because it was Harry.

If Stanley had something to do elsewhere in the hotel, Phyllis Dantagnon who managed the drugstore, or one of the other women, happily minded Harry. Until Beriker put an end to it. He ordered Harry out, telling Stanley that the hotel would no longer be a neighborhood country club, that it was going to be a world-class five-star hotel. Berkiker lost not only Harry, but Stanley as well.

People wondered how the sultan was planning to turn the hotel into this "world-class" establishment. Davis sold it before he could carry through on his $40 million promise to remodel. The hotel was in serious need of work. No one questioned that. The question was what would the sultan do?

The other question on some people's minds was, would the sultan ever appear in person? His brother's family came in great numbers, carried from Los Angeles International in a convoy of buses. Neighbors on Crescent Drive knew they were in town because the buses would be parked, with their motors, running near Bungalow 5.

Security men from the hotel waited at the airport to escort them up the freeway. Once a crisis arose when somehow the security men lost the buses at a stoplight. One moment the Bruneians were there, the next they were gone. Walkie-talkies squawked back and forth between the security men on the road and those back at the hotel, but no buses. After two hours, the buses pulled up at the hotel. Where had they been? On a buying spree at Toys 'R Us.

Leonard Stanley once saw a white Rolls Corniche convertible with its top down parked near one of the buses. After admiring it, he asked a doorman if it belonged to the sultan.

"Oh no, it belongs to one of the bodyguards."

Officially the sultan has never visited the hotel, although Leon Smith, who usually knows these things, says he came once, incognito.

There was some work being done at the hotel. The restaurant was redone, and enormous black and white photographs of stars were hung. Happier results were achieved when Bungalow 5 was renovated and refurbished for the Walter Annenbergs. A private pool and hot tub were added so Annenberg's friends, like Ronald Reagan, could come and go in privacy. (Annenberg was a longtime favorite with the staff for his generosity and kind gestures, such as coming out on the morning of December 25 to wish everyone a Merry Christmas.)

In 1991 the sultan bought Muriel Slatkin's 8,000-square-foot house and the lot next to it for $12.5 million in cash. The more than two acre purchase gave him complete possession of the "island" behind the hotel.

Muriel was not homeless for long. She bought a penthouse in the Wilshire House for $8.5 million. The apartment was even larger than her previous residence and had a master suite, guest suite, maid's quarters, two elevators, a gym, and a butler's pantry. The most remarkable—and people did remark—feature of the apartment was in the man's bathroom, a twelve-foot-high, black granite urinal. Anyone approaching it electronically activates a sheet of water that flows from the ceiling down the granite.

Finally the sultan showed his hand. Representatives of the hotel went to the city of Beverly Hills in November, 1991, in search of building permits and variances. There would, indeed, be a rejuvenation of the hotel, but it would be more than a facelift. The Beverly Hills was going to have major surgery from the inside out. There would be a new garage, a sumptuous head-of-state suite, the entrance and exit would be moved, bungalows gutted, and on and on to the tune of $150 million. The construction could take up to three years.

Since the hotel predated the incorporation of Beverly Hills, the city council had "never enacted a set of comprehensive regulations to address this unique area of the city." It probably wished it had done so when the city planning department was inundated with letters, many from neighbors opposed to the plans. Some railed against moving the entrance to Crescent Drive—the driveway had only kissed Crescent as it came off Sunset. They protested the increased traffic it would bring. Others decried the length of time the project would take, the noise and dirt it would create, and, the havoc it would bring to a residential neighborhood.

Some of the nearby homeowners retained lawyers. Barry Dean, who lived across the street from the hotel, estimated he spent between ten and fifteen thousand dollars on the case. A mergers and acquisitions specialist, Leonard Green,

whose house was across the alley, was one of the most vocif-
erous of the opponents. His lawyers from the high-powered
firm of Gibson, Dunn, & Crutcher, took the tactic that
regional planner George Sternlieb called the last in the
dance of the Seven Veils when trying to stop a project—cry
environmental damage. Green demanded an environmental
impact study, which had the potential of torpedoing the ren-
ovation altogether.

The neighbors weren't the only group crying foul. The
hotel workers' union couldn't get management to promise to
take back the employees when the hotel reopened. Charges
of "union-busting" were made. To add to the public-rela-
tions headache, a Beverly Hills resident, named Herb
Glaser, started an anti-Brunei campaign. In an interview in
the *Jewish Journal*, he denounced Brunei's voting record in
the United Nations, singling out its opposition to rescinding
the U.N. resolution that had equated Zionism with racism.
Events that would have been held at the hotel were booked
elsewhere.

In April 1992, Sajahtera requested that the planning
commission postpone consideration of the reconstruction
plans. "Ownership of the hotel is currently reassessing the
particulars of the proposed renovations. We will notify you
as soon as the ownership's reassessment is complete."

There was speculation that the sultan, or at least those
in his company, had soured on the hotel and wanted to dis-
pose of it before sinking a lot of money into the remodeling.
In August, Dan Dorfman reported as much in his *USA Today*
column. At almost the same time, the Beverly Hills City
Council was okaying the revised plan for a two-year reconstruction, during which time the hotel would be closed. The
neighbors had lost their lawsuit calling for an environmental
impact study.

The "specific plan" went into great detail on what was to be done and what couldn't be done, and it made many concessions to the neighbors' concerns—104 to be exact.

One of the provisions in the plan was the creation of a hotel-neighborhood liaison committee to deal with any complaints that might arise. The sultan also agreed to pay for a twenty-four-hour complaint line and a monitor to make sure the plan was being properly implemented.

Some of the items on the original "wish list," as Beriker called it, were expunged. No elaborate head-of-state suite, for one. But there would be central air conditioning (along with an air filtration system "to reduce any adverse air quality impacts on hotel employees and guests"), new wiring, plumbing, and heating. The number of rooms in the main building would be reduced by fifty-one to 210, and the number of parking spaces increased from 429 to 692. The sultan agreed to pay for employees to park at city or other lots, if there was not enough on-site space for them and provide free transportation to the hotel. (The employee licence plate numbers would be given to the city to keep the staff from parking on nearby streets.) The tennis court would be moved from next to the pool to the rear of the property, on top of a below-level parking facility. Bungalows could be enlarged, but by no more than 350 square feet. And the hotel would maintain the landscaping along Sunset Boulevard.

Importantly to those who cared about the Beverly Hills Hotel, the sultan was charged with preserving the "garden-resort" atmosphere. "The design of all renovations to the Beverly Hills Hotel will identify, perserve, and maintain the form and detailing of those materials and features that are important in defining the character of the Hotel...all renovations and construction shall be designed to preserve and enhance the mission revival heritage and other design styles of the original hotel."

The bell towers would stay. The tile roofs, as would the pink stucco, green and white stripes of the porte cochere, and the banana-leaf walls. And what must have made Nino Osti very happy, the Polo Lounge would not be changed.

Two years earlier the staff had been asked for input on what should be done to the hotel. Nino had written back, attempting to explain the importance of maintaining the Polo Lounge just as it was. "It wasn't built in a day. The shape of the tables are important. The room is just the right size; it works so well. If you're going to change things, change the air conditioning, put in a good filtering system. But don't change the pink lights. Ladies look best in this light. You know, they used to come in at night and put in new carpets and new chairs. No one noticed because they were exactly the same as the old ones."

The coffee shop would stay the same, as would the garden. As part of the plan, every tree, bush, flower, and vine was catalogued, eighty-three different ones—King Palms, Purple Orchid Trees, Persimmons, Weeping Chinese Banyans, Bougainvillea, Hibiscus, Southern Magnolia, a horticulturalist's delight. Only a few unhealthy plants would be removed.

Some of measures included to appease the neighbors were a ban on pile driving and power-actuated impact wrenches. There would be no excavation or exterior structural work done on the weekends or holidays. Tarps had to cover dirt being hauled from the site, and those trucks had to be cleaned before driving on to city streets.

If the reconstruction proceeds according to the timetable, it will be completed in two years.

Two years. That's a long time for a hotel to be closed. Guests would go to other hotels and get friendly with the staff. Would they return? Many guests had already abandoned the hotel. By the fall of 1992, the *Beverly Hills Courier* was putting the occupancy rate at a dismal 23 percent.

The few permanent guests had to find new places to live. Dave Tebet, the NBC executive who brought the Johnny Carson show to Los Angeles, left. Mark Goodson, who was suffering from cancer, told Nino Osti the hotel was like family to him. He didn't want changes at his age, even though he had been offered a house. Goodson died two weeks before the hotel closed.

The ailing industrialist Norton Simon and his wife Jennifer Jones, who had lived in Bungalow 9 for more than five years, had to relocate. Simon had been set to purchase a house a year earlier but had walked away from his nonrefundable $300,000 up-front money. The talk in town was that no decorator would work with Jones. Faced with the hotel closing, Simon found another house.

During the months leading up to the closing, only the tennis courts remained as busy as ever. (Patsy Klein, author of *Growing Up Spoiled in Beverly Hills*, a few years earlier had been wait-listed for what seemed like an eternity for the 8 a.m. Saturday time slot. Finally she got a call from one of the pros who had good news and bad news. The good news was Patsy finally had her desired court time, the bad was she had gotten it because the previous holder of the slot had committed suicide.)

Alien director Ridley Scott still took lessons. Eric Braeden, star of the soap *The Young and the Restless*, Charlton Heston and may others came to play.

Sven, who had returned after Davis left, was lonelier over at the pool. "There used to be a waiting list for cabana rentals. You could have one for the asking now." His eyes swept across what had been his domain for so long. "There used to be an excitement here. You felt it. Ava Gardner would be here and turn, and everyone would follow her movements. If someone said, there's so-and-so, you'd be blase, you'd seen so many, but it was exciting. It will never be that way again."

Many people were echoing similar thoughts as the closing neared.

Publicist Lee Solters lamented the closing. "It's a landmark and when it reopens, I hope it'll return to its glory, I really do. But we've had a lot of discussions among our friends in the motion picture industry, and two years is a long time. I remember when a restaurant named Ma Maison was the hangouts on Fridays. And then place closed. When it reopened nobody was there."

Even the weather in Los Angeles joined the mourning, with days of gloom and rain. A wastebasket stood at the entrance of the Polo Lounge to catch drips from the leaking roof. Most of the hotel was closed, and the few guests who arrived in those last weeks were housed in the Crescent Wing. There was little cheerful about the Beverly Hills Hotel. The staff knew that on the last day they would be given pink slips and asked to sign releases acknowledging they had been promised no future employment.

(Four assistant managers, including Nick Pappas and Elisa Danian, had already been fired. The previous January, not long after Christmans, they were called into Beriker's office, told to clear out their lockers and desks, and be out in two hours.)

A room service waiter who had worked there for eight years thought that ten people were retiring. "Everyone else is out looking. It's a very hard time. You go in, fill out the applications. They say there's nothing now. Then as soon as you leave, your application goes into the trash. Very hard, especially for those people with young children." His expression indicated he was one of them.

The official word was sent up from the front office. The hotel would be closed on December 30, at 2:00 p.m. Reading it, Nino Osti assumed there was a misprint. It should have been 2 a.m. That's when the Polo Lounge always closed. But no, management would gracelessly close the doors in the middle of the afternoon with "not even enough time for people to finish lunch."

Osti appealed for a more reasonable hour. In a compromise, it was agreed that the kitchen would close at six.

The timing of the closing seemed so arbitrary and foolish what with the Super Bowl scheduled for January 31 in Pasadena. Hotel rooms would be at a premium, and the last weekend the Super Bowl had been in the area, fourteen thousand people went through the Polo Lounge.

Apparently management didn't want any money on the books for 1993, so close the hotel would and close the hotel did on December 30.

The Polo Lounge had been completely booked for weeks, but it was not crowded on that last day. Realtor Kay Pick, who played in the pool sandbox as a child, said that many people had come by in the prior two weeks to say goodbye. "It was like a death in the family. A funeral."

Soon workmen would trod the halls where Garbo and Lombard, Monroe and Taylor had once walked. The sound of hammers and saws would replace the tinkle of ice and soft strains of Gershwin from the Polo Lounge's piano.

There would be tomorrows for the Beverly Hills Hotel, but they would never match its yesterdays.

afterword

The wooden barriers have gone up, but there is little sound of activity behind them. The whispers in town have started again. The sultan wants to sell. Someone offered him $50 million. Who would pay more when they know the hotel faces $100 million in restorations?

Will the doors of the Pink Palace stay closed forever?

Stay tuned.

March, 1993

index